p.

Alibis

ALSO BY ANDRÉ ACIMAN

FICTION
Eight White Nights
Call Me by Your Name

NONFICTION
Out of Egypt: A Memoir
False Papers: Essays on Exile and Memory
The Light of New York (with Jean-Michel Berts)
Entrez: Signs of France (with Steven Rothfield)

AS EDITOR
The Proust Project
*Letters of Transit: Reflections on Exile, Identity,
Language, and Loss*

Alibis

ESSAYS ON ELSEWHERE

André Aciman

FARRAR, STRAUS AND GIROUX ~ NEW YORK

Farrar, Straus and Giroux
18 West 18th Street, New York 10011

Copyright © 2011 by André Aciman
All rights reserved
Distributed in Canada by D&M Publishers, Inc.
Printed in the United States of America
First edition, 2011

Portions of this book have appeared, in slightly different form,
in *The American Scholar*; *Condé Nast Traveler*; *The Harvard Review*;
Horizons; *L'Espresso*; *The Light of New York*; *The New York Times*; *The New
York Times Magazine*; *Partisan Review*; *The Sophisticated Traveler*; *Tell Me
True: Memoir, History, Writing a Life*; and *The Threepenny Review*.

Library of Congress Cataloging-in-Publication Data
Aciman, André
    Alibis : essays on elsewhere / André Aciman.— 1st ed.
        p.   cm.
    ISBN 978-0-374-10275-3 (cloth : alk. paper)
    I. Title.

PS3601.C525 A79 2011
814'.6—dc22

                                                    2011010700

Designed by Jonathan D. Lippincott

www.fsgbooks.com

1   3   5   7   9   10   8   6   4   2

For Michael,
Hermosura

Contents

Alibis

Lavender

Life begins somewhere with the scent of lavender. My father is standing in front of a mirror. He has just showered and shaved and is about to put on a suit. I watch him tighten the knot of his necktie, flip down his shirt collar, and button it up. Suddenly, there it is, as always: lavender.

I know where it comes from. An elaborately shaped bottle sits on the dresser. One day, when I'm having a very bad migraine and am lying on the living room sofa, my mother, scrambling for something to take my mind off the pain, picks up the bottle, unscrews the cap, and dabs some of its contents onto a handkerchief, which she then brings to my nose. Instantly, I feel better. She lets me keep the handkerchief. I like to hold it in my fist, with my head tilted slightly back, as if I'd been punched in a fistfight and were still bleeding—or the way I'd seen others do when they were feeling sick or crushed and walked about the house taking occasional sniffs through crumpled handkerchiefs in what looked like last-ditch efforts to avoid a fainting spell. I liked the handkerchief, liked the secret scent emanating from within its folds, liked smuggling it to school and taking furtive whiffs in class, because the scent brought me back to my parents, to their living room, and into a world that was so serene that just inhaling its scent cast a protective cloud around me. Smell lavender and I was sheltered, happy, beloved. Smell lavender and in came good thoughts—about life, about those I loved, about me. Smell lavender and, no matter how far from one another, we were all gathered in one warm, snug room stuffed with pillows, close to a crackling fire, with the patter of rain outside to remind us our lives were secure. Smell lavender and you couldn't pull us apart.

My father's old cologne can be found the world over. I have only to walk into a large department store and there it is. Half a century later it looks exactly the same. I could, if I were prescient enough and did not want to risk walking into a store one day and not finding it, purchase a tiny bottle and keep it somewhere, as a stand-in for my father, for my love of lavender, or for that fall evening when, as an adolescent, I'd gone with my mother to buy my first aftershave but couldn't make up my mind and returned alone the next evening after school, happy to discover, among so many other things, that a man could use shaving as an excuse for wearing perfume.

I was baffled to find there were so many scents in the world, and even more baffled to find my father's scent among them. I asked the salesman to let me sample my father's brand, mispronouncing its name on purpose, overdoing my surprise as I examined its slanted shape as though it were a stranger whom I had hailed in error, knowing that the bottle and I were on intimate terms at home, that if it knew every twist my worst migraines took—as I knew every curve on its body—it knew of my imaginary flights from school in Mother's handkerchief, knew more about my fantasies than I dared know myself. And yet, in the shop that was about to close that day and whose owner was growing ever more impatient with my inability to choose, I felt mesmerized by something new, something at once dangerous and enticing, as though these numberless bottles, neatly arranged in stacks around the store, held the promise of nights out in large cities where everything from the buildings, lights, faces, foods, places, and the bridges I'd end up crossing made the world ever more desirable, if only because I too, by virtue of this or that potion, had become desirable—to others, to myself.

I spent an hour testing bottles. In the end I bought a lavender cologne, but not my father's. After paying and having the package gift wrapped, I felt as though I'd been handed a birth certificate or a new passport. This would be me—or me as long as the bottle lasted. Then we'd have to look into the matter again.

Over time, I discovered all kinds of lavenders. There were light, ethereal lavenders; some were mild and timid; others lush and overbearing; some tart, as if picked from the field and left to parch in large vats of vinegar; others were overwhelmingly sweet. Some lavenders ended up smelling like an herb garden; others, with hints of so many spices, were blended beyond recognition.

I experimented with each one, purchased many bottles, not just because I wanted to collect them all or was searching for the ideal lavender—the hidden lavender, the ur-lavender that superseded all other lavenders—but because I was eager to either prove or disprove something I suspected all along: that the lavender I wanted was none other than the one I'd grown up with and would ultimately turn back to once I'd established that all the others were wrong for me. Perhaps the lavender I wanted was basic lavender. Ordinary lavender. Papa's lavender. You go out into the world to acquire all manner of habits and learn all sorts of languages, but the one tongue you neglect most is the one you've spoken at home, just as the customs you feel most comfortable with are those you never knew were customs until you saw others practice completely different ones and realized you didn't quite mind your own, though you'd strayed so far now that you probably no longer knew how to practice them. I collected every fragrance in the world. But my scent—what was *my* scent? Had I ever had a *scent*? Was there going to be one scent only, or would I want all of them?

What I found after purchasing several aftershaves was that they would all lose their luster, like certain elements in the actinide series that have a brief radioactive life before turning into lead. Some smelled too strong, or too weak, or too much of such and such and not enough of this or that. Some failed to bring out something essential about me; others suggested things that weren't in me at all. Perhaps finding fault with each fragrance was also my way of finding fault with myself, not just for choosing the wrong fragrance each time, or for even thinking I needed a fragrance in the first place, but for believing that the blessings conferred by cologne could ever bring about the new life I yearned for.

And yet, even as I criticized each fragrance, I found myself growing attached to it, as though something that had less to do with the fragrances themselves than with that part of me that had sought them out and been seduced by them and finally blossomed because of them should never be allowed to perish. Sometimes the history of provisional attachments means more to us than the attachments themselves, the way the history of a love affair stirs more love than the affair itself. Sometimes it is in blind ritual and not faith that we encounter the sacred, the way it is habit not character that makes us who we are. Sometimes the clothes and scents we wear have more of us in them than we do ourselves.

The search for ideal lavender was like the search for that part of me that needed nothing more than a fragrance to emerge from the sleep of thousands. I searched for it the way I searched for my personal color, or for a brand of cigarettes, or for my favorite composer. Finding the right lavender would finally allow me to say, "Yes, this is me. Where was I all this time?" Yet, no sooner is the scent purchased, than the me who was supposed to emerge—like the us who is about to emerge when we buy new clothes, or sign up for a magazine that seems so thoroughly right for us, or purchase a membership to a health club, or move to a new city, or discover a new faith and practice new rituals with new congregants among whom we make new friends—this me turns out to be, of course, the one we'd always wished to mask or drive away. What did I expect? Different scent, same person.

Over the past thirty-five years I have tried almost all the colognes and aftershaves that perfume manufacturers have concocted. Not just lavenders, but pine, chamomile, tea, citrus, honeysuckle, fern, rosemary, and smoky variations of the most rarefied leathers and spices. I liked nothing more than to clutter my medicine cabinet and the entire rim of my bathtub with bottles two and three deep, each vial like a tiny, unhatched effigy of someone I was, or wished to be, and, for a while, thought I'd finally become. Scent A: purchased in such and such a year, hoping to encounter happiness. Scent B: purchased while scent A was almost finished; it helped me abandon A. C, marking sudden fatigue with B. D was a gift. Never liked it; wore it to make the giver happy; stopped using it as soon as she was gone. Comes E, which I loved so much that I eventually purchased F, along with nine of its sibling scents made by the same house. Yet F managed to make me tire of E and its isotopes. Sought out G. Disliked it as soon as I realized that someone I hated loved it. Then H. How I loved H! Stayed with H for years. They don't make it any longer; should have stocked up on it. But then, much as I loved it, I had stopped using it long before its manufacturer discontinued it. Back to E, which I had always liked. Yes, definitely E. Until I realized there had always been something slightly off, something missing about E. I stopped using it again. Of the woman who breezed through my life and, in the ten days I knew her, altered me forever, all I remember is her gift. I continued to wear the fragrance she'd given me as a way of thinking she'd be back soon enough. Now, twenty years later, all that's left of her is a bottle that reminds me less of her than of the lover I once was.

I have thrown many things away in life. But aftershave bottles, never. I take these bottles wherever I move, the way the ancients traveled with their ancestral masks. Each bottle contains a part of

me, the formaldehyded me, the genie of myself. One could, as in an
Arabian tale, rub each bottle and summon up an earlier me. Some,
despite the years, are still alive, though not a thing they own or
wear is any longer in my possession; others have even died or grown
so dull I want nothing more to do with them; I've forgotten their
phone number, their favorite song, their furtive wishes. I take up an
old scent and, suddenly, I remember why this scent always reminds
me of the most ardent days of my life—ardent not because they had
been happy times, but because I had spent so much time thirsting
for happiness that, in retrospect, some of that imagined happiness
must have rubbed off and scented an entire winter, casting a happy
film over days I've always known I'd never wish to relive. And as I
hold this bottle, which seems more precious than so many things,
I begin to think that one day someone I love—particularly someone
I love—will happen along and open it and wonder what this scent
could possibly have meant to me. What was it I'd wished to keep
alive all these years? This is the scent of early spring when they
called to say things had gone my way. This of an evening with my
mother, when she came to meet me downtown and I thought how
old she looks—now I realize she was younger by ten years than I am
today. This the night of the A-minor. "And this?" they'll want to
ask. "How about this one?"

Fragrances linger for decades, and our loved ones may remember us by them, but the legend in each vial clams up the moment we're gone. Our genie speaks to no one. He simply watches
as those he's loved open and investigate. He's dying to scream
with the agony of ten Rosetta stones begging to be heard across
the centuries. "This was the day I discovered pleasure. And this—
how couldn't any of you know?—this was the night we met, standing outside Carnegie Hall after a concert, and how simply one
thing led to another, and afterward, when it rained, we had waited
awhile under the cantilever, both reluctant to leave, having found
a pretext in rain, strangers starting to talk, making a quick dash

into a nearby coffee shop—deplorable coffee, damp shoes, wet hair, surly foreign waiter mumbling Unspeakanese when we tipped him kindly—and sat and spoke of Mahler and *The Four Quartets*, and no one would have guessed, not even us, we'd end up together in a studio on the Upper West Side." But the voice cannot be heard. To die is to forget you ever lived. To die is to forget you loved, or suffered, or got and lost things you wanted. Tomorrow, you say to yourself, I won't remember anything, won't remember this face, this knee, this old scar, or the hand that wrote all this.

The bottles are stand-ins for me. I keep them the way the ancient Egyptians kept all of their household belongings: for that day when they'd need them in their afterlife. To part with them now is to die before my time. And yet, there are times when I think there should have been many, many other bottles there—not just bottles I lost or forgot about, but bottles I never owned, bottles I didn't even know existed and, but for a tiny accident, might have given an entirely different scent to my life. There is a street I pass by every day, never once suspecting that in years to come it will lead to an apartment I still don't know will be mine one day. How can I not know this—isn't there a science?

Conversely, there are places I bid farewell to long before knowing I must leave, places and people whose disappearance I rehearse not just to learn how to live without them when the time comes but to put off their loss by foreseeing it a bit at a time beforehand. I live in the dark so as not to be blinded when darkness comes. I do the same with life, making it more conditional and provisional than it already is, so as to forget that one day my birthday will come around and I won't be there to celebrate it.

It is still unthinkable that those who caused us the greatest pain and turned us inside out could at some point in time have been totally unknown, unborn to us. We might have crossed them in numberless places, given them street directions, opened a door for them, stood up to let them take their seat in a crowded concert hall, and never once recognized the person who would ruin us for everyone else. I'd be willing to shave years from the end of my life to go back and intercept that evening under a cantilever when we both put our coats over our heads and rushed through the rain after coffee and I said, almost without thinking, I didn't want to say good night yet, although it was already dawn. I would give years, not to unwrite this evening or to rewrite it, but to put it on hold and, as happens when we bracket off time, be able to wonder indefinitely who I'd be had things taken another turn. Time, as always, is given in the wrong tense.

The walls of the Farmaceutica of Santa Maria Novella in Florence are lined with rows of tiny drawers, each of which contains a different perfume. Here I could create my own scent museum, my own laboratory, my imaginary Grasse, the perfume capital of France, with all its quaint ateliers and narrow lanes and winding passageways linking one establishment to the next. My scent museum would boast even its own periodic table, listing all the perfumes in my life, beginning, of course, with the first, the simplest, the lightest—lavender, the hydrogen of all fragrances—followed by the second, the third, the fourth, each standing next to the other like milestones in my life, as though there were indeed a method to the passage of time. In the place of helium (He, atomic number 2) I'd have Hermès, and in the place of lithium (Li, 3) Liberty; Bernini would replace beryllium (Be, 4), Borsari boron (B, 5), Carven carbon (C, 6), Night nitrogen (N, 7), Onyx oxygen (O, 8), and Floris fluorine (F, 9). And before I know it my entire life could be charted by these elements alone: Arden instead of argon (Ar, 18), Knize instead of potassium (K, 19), Canoe for calcium (Ca, 20), Guerlain for germanium (Ge, 32), Yves Saint Laurent for yttrium (Y, 39), Patou for platinum (Pt, 78), and, of course, Old Spice for osmium (Os, 76).

As in Mendeleyev's periodic table, one could sort these scents in rows and categories: by herbs, flowers, fruits, spices, woods. Or by places. By people. By loves. By the hotels where this or that soap managed to cast an unforgettable scent over this or that great city. By the films or foods or clothes or concerts we've loved. By perfumes women wore. Or even by years, so that I could mark the bottles as my grandmother would when she labeled each jar of marmalade with her neat octogenarian's cursive, noting on each the fruit and the year of its make—as though each scent had its own *Werke-Verzeichnis* number. Aria di Parma (1970), Acqua Amara (1975), Ponte Vecchio (1980).

The aftershaves I used at 18 and at 24, different fragrances, yet located on the same column: a voyage to Italy is what they shared. Me at 16 and me at 32: twice the age, yet still nervous when calling a woman for the first time; at 40 I couldn't solve the calculus problems I didn't understand at 20; after rereading and teaching *Wuthering Heights* so many times, the scenes I remembered best at 48 were those retained from my very first reading at 12, four "generations" earlier. Me at 14, 18, 22, 26—life retold in units of four. Me at 21, 26, 31, 36, of fives. The folio method, the quarto method, the octavo—in halves, in fourths, by eighths. Life arranged in Fibonacci's sequence: 8, 13, 21, 34, 55, 89. Or in Pascal's: 4, 10, 20, 35, 56. Or by primes: 7, 11, 13, 17, 19, 23, 29, 31. Or in combinations of all three: I was handsome at 21, why did I think I wasn't; I had so much going for me at 34, why then was I longing to be who I'd been at 17? At 17, I couldn't wait to be 23. At 23, I longed to meet the girls I'd known at 17. At 51, I'd have given anything to be 35, and at 41 was ready to dare things I was unprepared for at 23. At 20, 30 seemed the ideal age. At 80, will I manage to think I'm half my age? Will there be summer in the snow?

Time's covenants are all warped. We live Fibonacci lives: three steps forward, two steps back, or the other way around: three steps forward, five back. Or in both directions simultaneously, in the manner of spiders or of Bach's crab canons, spinning combinations of

scents and elective affinities in what turns out to be an endless
succession of esters and fragrances that start from the simplest
and fan out to the most complex: one carbon, two carbons, three
carbons; six hydrogens, eight hydrogens, ten . . . $C_3H_6O_2$, ethyl
formate; $C_4H_8O_2$, ethyl acetate; $C_5H_{10}O_2$, ethyl propionate; $C_5H_{10}O_2$,
methyl butanoate (which has an apple aroma); $C_5H_{10}O_2$, propyl
ethanoate (pear aroma); $C_6H_{12}O_2$, ethyl butyrate; $C_7H_{14}O_2$, ethyl
valerate (banana); $C_8H_9NO_2$, methyl anthranilate (grape); $C_9H_{10}O_2$,
benzylyl ethanoate (peach); $C_{10}H_{12}O_2$, ethyl phenyl ethanoate
(honey); $C_{10}H_{20}O_2$, octyl ethanoate (orange-apricot); $C_{11}H_{24}O_2$,
ethyl decanoate (cognac); $C_9H_6O_2$, coumarin (lavender). Say lavender and you have a scent, a chain, a lifetime.

And here lay Mendeleyev's genius. He understood that, though
he could plot every element, many elements hadn't been discovered yet. So he left blank spaces on his table—for missing elements,
for elements to come—as though life's events were cast in so orderly
and idealized a numerical design that, even if we ignored when
they'd occur or what effect they might have, we could still await
them, still make room for them before their time. Thus, I too look
at my life and stare at its blind spots: scents I never discovered;
bottles I haven't stumbled on and don't know exist; selves I haven't
been but can't claim to miss; pockets in time I should have but
never did live through; people I could have met but missed out
on; places I might have visited, gotten to love, and ultimately
lived in, but never traveled to. They are the blank tiles, the "rare-
earth" moments, the roads never taken.

II

There is another fragrance, a woman's perfume. No one I know
has ever worn it. So there is no one to associate it with.

I discovered it one fall evening on my way home after a

graduate seminar. In Cambridge, Massachusetts, there is a high-end drugstore on Brattle Street, and sometimes, perhaps to daw-dle and not head home sooner than I had to, I'd take the long way and stop inside. I liked Brattle Street around Harvard Square, especially in the early evening when the shops were all aglow and people were coming back from work, running last-minute er-rands, some with children in tow, the bustling traffic of people giving the sidewalks a heady feel I grew to love, if only because it seemed rife with prospects for the evening I already knew were false. The sidewalk was the only place I felt at home in this oth-erwise cold, anonymous part of town where I wasted so much time and so many years alone, and where everyone I knew always seemed so very busy doing such small things. I missed home, missed people, hated being alone, missed having tea, had tea alone to invoke the presence of someone over tea.

On such evenings the Café Algiers was always crowded. It was good to drink tea with strangers, even if one didn't talk to them. A ziggurat of Twinings tins stood on a cluttered counter behind the cash register. I would eventually try each tea, from Darjeeling to Formosa oolong to Lapsang souchong and gunpowder green. I liked the idea of tea more than the flavors themselves, the way I liked the idea of tobacco more than of smoking, of people more than of friendship, of home more than my apartment on Craigie Street.

The pharmacy stood at the end of a stretch of stores near the corner of Church Street. It was the last spot before I'd turn and head home. I stepped in one evening. Inside, I discovered an en-tirely different world from the one I'd imagined. The tiny pharmacy was filled with luxury beauty products, luxury perfumes, shampoos of all nations, Old World soaps, balms, lotions, striped toothbrushes, badgers, old-empire shaving creams. I liked it in there. The antique cabinets, the ancient wares, the whole obsolescence of the shop, down to its outdated razors and aging, Central European owners, all seemed welcoming, solicitous. So I asked—because you couldn't loiter without buying something—for an aftershave I thought they wouldn't have, only to find that they not only carried it but also sold its many companion products. So I was obliged to buy something I had stopped using a decade earlier.

A few days later I was back, not just because the pharmacy helped put off my unavoidable walk home, or because I wished to repeat the experience of opening a door and lighting upon a universe of bygone toiletries, but because the store had itself become a last stop in an imaginary Old World, before that world turned into what it really was: Cambridge.

I came again early one evening after seeing a French film at the Brattle Theater. During the showing, it had started to snow outside, and the snow, fast piling on Cambridge, gave every sign of turning into a blizzard that night. A luminous halo hung over Brattle Street just outside the theater, as it had in the small town of Clermont-Ferrand in the movie. In the near-total absence of traffic, some neighborhood children had gathered outside the Casablanca restaurant with their sleds and were about to head down toward the Charles River. I envied them.

I did not want to go home. Instead, I decided to trundle over to my pharmacy. It seemed as good a destination as any. I pushed in the glass door as fast as I could, stamping my feet outside before taking shelter within. A young blond woman with a boy of about four was standing inside, holding a handkerchief to her son's nose. The boy made an effort to blow but wasn't successful. The mother smiled at him, at the salesgirl, at me, almost by way of apology, then folded the handkerchief and applied it to his nose again. "*Noch einmal,*" she added. The boy, sticking his head out of a red hood, blew. "*Noch einmal,*" she repeated with a tone of gentle entreaty, which reminded me of my own mother when she implored me to do things that were good for me, her voice filled with so vast a store of patience that it suddenly reminded me of how distant I'd grown from the love of others. Within moments, a cold whiff of air blew into the store. The mother had opened the door and, with her child bundled up, walked out into the snow.

Only the salesgirl and I were left. Perhaps because she was no longer in the mood for business on such a spellbound evening, or because it was almost closing time, the salesgirl, who knew me by then, said she would let me smell something really special, and named a perfume.

Had I heard of it? I thought I had—on second thought, I wasn't sure. She ignored my attempted fib, and proceeded to open a tiny vial. Having moistened the glass stopper with the perfume, she dabbed it on her skin and in a gesture that made me think she was about to caress me on the cheek—which wouldn't have surprised me, because I'd always felt she had a weakness for me, which was also why I'd come back—she brought an exposed smooth wrist gently to my lips, which I would have kissed on impulse if I hadn't already seen the gesture performed at perfume counters.

No fragrance I'd ever known before smelled anything remotely similar to this. I was at once in Thailand and in France and on a vessel bound for the Bosporus with women who wore furs in the summer and spoke of Webern's *Langsamer Satz* as they turned to me and whispered *"Noch einmal?"* It eclipsed every fragrance I'd known. It had lavender, but lavender derealized, deferred, dissembled, which is why I asked her to let me smell her wrist again, but she'd seen through my request, and wasn't sure, as I wasn't sure, that it was limited to perfume alone. Instead, she dabbed the bottle stopper on a scent strip, which she snapped out of a tiny wad filled with other strips, waved the paper ever so lightly in the air to let it dry, and then handed it to me, with a look of complicity that suggested she wasn't about to be fooled by my curiosity and had already guessed that there were at least two women in my life who'd want nothing more than to see the scent strip I'd bring home that evening turn into a gift vial within days. That look flattered me no end.

I came back two evenings later, and then again, not for the store now, not for the snow, or for the elusive luster that hovered over Brattle Street in the evening, but for the revelation in that perfume bottle, for the women in furs who smoked Balkans aboard a yacht while watching the Hellespont drift in the distance. I did not even know whether the perfume was my reason for being in there or whether it had become an excuse, the mask behind the mask, because if it was the salesgirl I was after, or the women that the flicker in her eyes had invoked, I also felt that behind her was the image of another woman, my mother, in another perfume store, though I sensed that she too, perhaps, was nothing more than a mask, behind which was my father, years and years ago now, as he stood by the mirror, pleased to be the man he was when he dabbed lavender water on his cheeks after shaving. He too, like all the others now, reduced to a threadbare mask for the love and the happiness I was trying to find and despaired I'd never know. The scent summoned me like a numinous mirage from across a divide so difficult to cross that I thought it might not have anything to do with love either, for love couldn't be the source of so much hardship, and therefore perhaps that love itself was a mask, and that if it wasn't love I was after, then the very tip of this vortex around which I'd been circling had to do with me—just me—but a me that was squandered on so many spaces, and on so many layers, that it shifted like mercury the moment I touched it, or hid away like lanthanides, or flared up only to turn into the dullest substance a moment later.

The perfume was so expensive that all I could take with me, after coming up with more excuses, which seemed to prove to the salesgirl that there *were* other women in my life, was a sprinkle on a paper strip. I kept the strip with me, as if it belonged to someone who had gone away for a while and wouldn't forgive me if I didn't sniff it each day.

About a week later, after seeing the same film, I rushed out of the theater and headed toward the pharmacy, only to find that it had already closed. I stayed around for a few minutes, thinking back to the evening when I'd seen the mother and son there, remembering her blond hair bundled under her hat and her eyes that had roamed around the store and lingered on mine while she urged her son on, sensing I both wanted and envied her. Had she overplayed her maternal gaze to forestall any attempt at conversation? Had the salesgirl intercepted my glance?

Now I pictured mother and son coming out of the store, the mother struggling to open her umbrella on Church Street as they headed toward the Cambridge Common, plodding across the empty field with their colored boots sinking deep into the snow, their backs forever turned to me. It felt so real, and they seemed to disappear with such haste as the wind gusted at their backs that I caught an impulse to cry out with the only words I knew: "Frau Noch Einmal . . . Frau Noch Einmal . . ."

At the time I thought they were an imaginary wife and an imaginary son, the ones I so desperately wished might be mine one day. Me coming back from work and getting off at Harvard Square, she on a last-minute errand before dinner, buying him a toy at the drugstore because she'd promised him one that morning—*So what if we spoiled him a bit! Just fancy, running into each other in the snow, on this day of all days.* But now, through the distance of years, I think she may have been my mother, and the little boy, me. Or perhaps all this is, as ever, a mask. I was both me and my father, me as a student who'd gone to the movies instead of the library, me as the boy's better father, who'd probably have let him savor childhood a bit longer, me in the future giving the boy vague tips about things to come, all of it reminding me that the crib notes we sneak through time are written in invisible ink.

The boy from the pharmacy is thirty years old today—five years older than I was on the day I felt old enough to be his father. Yet, if I am younger still today than he is at thirty, I was on that day in the snow far older than either of us is today.

From time to time I revisit that perfume, especially when I wade through the cosmetics counters on the first floor of large department stores. Invariably I play dumb—"What's this?" I ask, playing the hapless husband trying to buy a last-minute gift. And they tell me, and they spray it for me, and they give me sample strips, which I stick in my coat pocket, and take them out, and put them back in, dreaming back to those days when I dreamt of a life I'm no longer sure I lived.

Perhaps fragrance is the ultimate mask, the mask between me and the world, between me and me, the other me, the shadow me I trail and get hints of but cannot know, sensing all along that talk of another me is itself the most insidious mask of all. But then perhaps fragrance is nothing more than a metaphor for the "no" I brought to everything I saw when I could so easily have said "yes"—to myself, to my father, to life—perhaps because I never loved any of the things of the world well enough and hoped to hide this fact from myself by thinking I could do better by looking elsewhere, or because I loved and wanted each fragrance and couldn't determine which to settle for, and therefore stored the very best till a second life rolled in. As irony would have it, the one perfume I want is the one I never purchased. It is also the one every woman I've known has cunningly refused to wear. So there is no one to remember it by. The perfume conjures an imagined life, it conjures no one.

Last winter I returned to the same pharmacy with my nine-year-old son. We did the rounds, as I always do nowadays whenever I go back to places I've spun too many yarns over to even bother wondering whether I've ever loved them or not. As usual, I pretend to be looking for a perfume for my wife. "Do you think Mom would like this one?" I ask my son, hoping he'll say no, which he does. I apologize. We look at toothbrushes, soaps, ancient tooth-

pastes; even my father's aftershave sits before me,
with reproof. I let him smell it. He likes it. I ask whe~
ognizes it. He does. We sample another. He likes that on~
is, I catch myself hoping, making his own memories.

Finding nothing to buy, we open the glass door and leav
Taking a quick right, we walk toward the Common. I try to tell
him that I'd once had a glimpse of him there almost three decades
ago. He looks at me as if I'm crazy. Or was it just me I'd seen decades ago, I ask. This is crazy too, he says. I want to tell him about
Frau Noch Einmal, but I can't find the right words. Instead I tell
him I am glad he is with me. He cracks a joke. I crack one back.

But I stop all the same and stand a moment on the very same
spot and remember the night I'd nearly shouted *Noch einmal* to
the winds on the snowed-on, empty Cambridge streets, thinking
of the German woman and of her lucky husband coming back
from work every evening. Here, at twenty-five, I had conjured the
life I wished to live one day. Now, at fifty, I was revisiting the life
I'd dreamed of living.

Had I lived it? Had I lived my life? And which mattered more
and which did I recall best: the one I'd dreamed up or the one I
indeed led? Or am I already forgetting both before my time, with
life taking back, one by one, the things I thought were mine to
keep, turning the cards face down, one by one, to deal someone
else another hand?

La Bouilladisse, June 2001

The house where we're staying near Aix-en-Provence is surrounded by lavender bushes that seem to billow and wave whenever a wind courses through the fields. Tomorrow is our last day
in Provence, and we've already washed all our clothes to let them
dry in the sun. I know that the next time I'll put on this shirt
will be in Manhattan. I know too how the scent of sunlight and

avender trapped within its folds will bring me back to this most luminous day in Provence.

It is ten o'clock in the morning and I am standing in this garden next to a wicker hamper that is filled with today's wash. My wife doesn't know it yet, but I've decided to hang the laundry myself. It's meant as a surprise. I've already brewed coffee.

So here I am, hanging one towel after the other, the boys' underwear, their many T-shirts, their socks flecked with the reddish clay from Roussillon which, I hope, will never wash off. I like the smell. I like separating the shirts on the line, leaving no more than half an inch between them. I must manage my pins and use them sparingly, making sure I'll have enough for the whole load. I know my wife will still find something to criticize in my method. The thought amuses me. I like the work, its mind-numbing pace that makes everything seem so simple, so complacent. I want it never to end. I can see why people take forever to hang clothes out to dry. I like the smell of parched wood on the clothespins, which are stored in a clay pot. I like the smell of clay too. I like the sound of drops trickling from our large towels onto the pebbles, on my feet. I like standing barefoot, like the sheets, which take forever to hang evenly and need three pins, one at each end and one for good measure in the middle. I turn around and, before picking up another shirt, I run my fingers through a stalk of lavender nearby. How easy it is to touch lavender. To think I fussed so much and for so long—and yet here it is, given to me, the way gold was given to the Incas, who didn't think twice before handing it over to strangers. There is nothing to want here. *Quod cupio mecum est.* What I want, I already have.

Yesterday we went to see the abbey of Sénanque. I took pictures of my sons standing in front of a field of lavender. From a distance, the lavender is so dark it looks like a bruise upon a sea of green. Closer by, each plant looks like an ordinary overgrown bush. I taught them how to rub their hands along lavender blossoms without disturbing the bees. We spoke of Cistercian monks and the production of dyes, of spirits, balms, and scented extracts, and of Saint Bernard de Clairvaux, and of medieval commerce routes that still exist today and that spread from these tiny abbeys to the rest of the world. For all I know my love of lavender may have started right here, in an essence gathered from bushes that grow on these very same fields. For all I know this is where it ends, in the beginning. And yet, for all I know, everything could start all over again—my father, my mother, the girl with the perfumed wrist, Frau Noch Einmal, her little boy, my little boy, myself as a little boy, the walk in the evening snow, the genie in the bottle, the Rosetta stone within each one of us that nothing, not even love or friendship, can unburden, the life we think of each day, and the life not lived, and the life half lived, and the life we wish we'd learn to live while we still have time, and the life we want to rewrite if only we could, and the life we know remains unwritten and may never be written at all, and the life we hope others may live far better than we have, all of it, for all I know, braided on one thread into which is spun something as simple as the desire to be one with the world, to find something instead of nothing, and having found something, never to let go, be it even a stalk of lavender.

Intimacy

I finally went back to Via Clelia. I had passed by the first time I
returned to Rome almost forty years ago, then a second time fifteen years later, and still another three years after that. But for
reasons that had more to do with my reluctance to come back here,
these visits occurred either by night, when I couldn't see a thing,
or when I didn't dare ask our cabby to make a right and stall
awhile to let me see our old home again. From Via Appia Nuova,
a bustling working-class artery, all I ever caught was a distant
glimpse of Via Clelia. After that third time, I stopped trying. In
Rome, whenever I go back, I never venture beyond the center.

Summer before last, though, with my wife and sons, I took
the Metro and got off at the Furio Camillo stop, two blocks north
of Via Clelia, exactly as I'd always envisaged the visit. Two blocks
would give me plenty of time to settle into the experience, gather
my impressions, and unlock memory's sluice gates, one by one—
without effort, caution, or ceremony. Two blocks, however, would
also allow me to put up whatever barriers needed to come up
between me and this lower-middle-class street whose grimy, ill-
tempered welcome, when we landed in Italy as refugees more
than four decades ago, I've never managed to forget.

I had meant to enter Via Clelia precisely where it crosses Via
Appia Nuova and take my time recognizing the streets, whose
names are drawn from Virgil mostly—Via Enea, Via Camilla, Via
Eurialo, Via Turno—and confer far-fetched echoes of imperial

grandeur on this rinky-dink quarter. I had meant to touch minor signposts along the way: the printer's shop (still there), the make-shift grocer-*pizzaiolo*, the one or two corner bars, the plumber (gone), the barbershop across the street (gone too), the tobacco-nist, the tiny brothel where you didn't dare look in when the two old frumps left their door ajar, the spot where a frail street singer would stand every afternoon and bellow out bronchial arias you strained to recognize, only to hear, when his dirge was done, a scatter of coins rain upon the sidewalk.

Home was right above his spot.

As I began walking down Via Clelia with my wife and sons, pointing out aspects of a street I'd known so well during the three years I'd lived there with my parents while we waited for visas to America, I caught myself hoping that no one I knew back then would be alive today, or, if they were, that none might recognize me. I wanted to give no explanations, answer no questions, embrace no one, touch or get close to nobody. I had always been ashamed of Via Clelia, ashamed of its good people, ashamed of having lived among them, ashamed of myself now for feeling this way, ashamed, as I told my sons, of how I'd always misled my private-school classmates into thinking I lived "around" the affluent Appia Antica and not in the heart of the blue-collar Appia Nuova. That shame had never gone away; shame never does, it was there on every corner of the street. Shame, which is the reluctance to be who we're not even sure we are, could end up being the deepest thing about us, deeper even than who we are, as though beyond identity were buried reefs and sunken cities teeming with creatures we couldn't begin to name because they came long before us. All I really wanted, as we began walking to the other end of Via Clelia, was to put the experience behind me now—*We've done Via Clelia*, I'd say—knowing all along that I wouldn't mind a sudden flare-up of memory to make good the visit.

Torn between wanting the whole thing over and done with

and wanting perhaps to feel something, I began to make light of
our visit with my sons. Fancy spending three years in this dump.
And the stench on hot summer days. On this corner I saw a dead
dog once; he'd been run over and was bleeding from both ears.
And here, every afternoon, sitting cross-legged on the sidewalk
by the tramway stop, a young Gypsy used to beg, her bare, dark
knee flaunted boldly over her printed skirt—savage, dauntless,
shameless. On Sunday afternoons Via Clelia was a morgue. In the
summer the heat was unbearable. In the fall, coming back after
school on the number 85 bus, I'd run errands for Mother, always
rushing back out of the apartment before the shops closed, and by
early twilight, watch the salesgirls head home, and always think
of Joyce's "Araby." The girl at the tiny supermarket down the
street, the salesgirls of the tiny local department store, the girl at
the butcher's who always extended credit when money was tight
toward the end of every month.

There was a girl who came every day for vitamin B_{12} shots.
My mother, once a volunteer nurse during World War II, was only
too glad to administer the injections; it gave her something to do.
Afterward, the girl and I would sit and talk in the kitchen till it
was time for dinner. Then she disappeared down the staircase.
Gina. The landlady's daughter. I never felt the slightest desire for
Gina, but it was kinder to conceal what I couldn't feel behind
a veil of feigned timidity and inexperience. Neither timidity nor
inexperience were feigned in the slightest, of course, but I exaggerated the performance to suggest a dissembled feint somewhere and that behind it lurked a waggish side capable of great
mischief if given the go-ahead. I feigned an earnest, bashful gaze
the better to hide the writhing diffidence underneath.

With the girl in the supermarket, it was the other way around.
I couldn't hold her gaze and was compelled each time to affect the
arrogance of someone who might have stared one day but had
forgotten to the next.

I hated my shyness. I wanted to hide it, but there was nothing to hide it with. Even trying to cover it up brought out more blushes and made me more flustered yet. I learned to hate my eyes, my height, my accent. To speak to a stranger, or to the girl at the supermarket, or to anyone for that matter, I needed to shut down everything about me, weigh my words, plan my words, affect a makeshift *romanaccio* to cover up my foreign accent, and, to avoid making any grammar mistakes in Italian, start undoing every sentence before I'd even finished speaking it and, because of this, end up making worse mistakes, the way some writers change the course of a sentence while still writing it but forget to remove all traces of where it was originally headed, thereby speaking with more than one voice. I dissembled with everyone—with those I wanted nothing from, with those I wanted anything they could give if only they could help me ask. I dissembled what I thought, what I feared, who I was, who I wasn't even sure I was.

Wednesday evenings, I remember, were earmarked for running errands and redeeming bottles at the tiny supermarket at the end of Via Clelia. The girl in charge of stacking the shelves would come to the back counter and help me with the bottles. I was scared each time I watched her empty the bag of bottles fast, feeling that time was flitting by sooner than I'd hoped. My gaze seemed to upset her, because she always lost her smile when she stared at me. Hers was the dark, ill-tempered stare of someone who was trying not to be rude. With other men, she was all smiles and bawdy jokes. With me, just the glare.

We arrived at the Furio Camillo Metro station at ten in the morning. At 10:00 a.m. in late July I'd be in my room upstairs, probably reading. On occasion, we'd go to the beach before it grew too hot. But past the third week of the month, the money ran out and we'd stay indoors, listening to the radio, saving the money for an occasional movie on weekday evenings, when tickets at the seedy and deserted third-run movie theater around the corner were cheaper than on Sundays. There were two movie theaters. One had disappeared; the other, all gussied up now, stands on Via Muzio Scevola, named after the early-Roman hero who burned his right hand on realizing he'd murdered the wrong man. One night, in that theater, a man put his hand on my wrist. I asked him what was the matter with him, and soon enough he moved to another seat. In those days, I told my sons, you also learned to avoid the bathrooms in movie theaters.

One more block and scarcely five minutes after arriving, our visit was over. This always happens when I go back to places. Either buildings shrink over time, or the time it takes to revisit them shrinks to less than five minutes. We had walked from one end of the street to the other. There was nothing more to do now but walk back the way we came. I sensed, from the way my wife and sons were waiting for me to tell them what to do next, that they were glad the visit was over. On our way back up the street, I did spend a few more seconds standing before the building, not just to take the moment in and never say I'd rushed or bungled the experience, but because I still hoped that an undisclosed something might rush out and tug me, exclaiming, as some people do when they suddenly show up at your door after many years, "Remember me?" But nothing happened. I was, as I always am during such moments, numb to the experience.

Writing about it—after the fact, as I did later that day—might eventually un-numb me. Writing, I was sure, would dust off things that were not there at the time of my visit, or that were there but that I wasn't quite seeing and needed time and paper to sort out, so that, once written about, they'd confer on my visit the retrospective resonance that part of me had hoped to find here on Via Clelia. Writing might even bring me closer to this street than I'd been while living there. Writing wouldn't alter or exaggerate anything; it would simply excavate, rearrange, lace a narrative, recollect in tranquility, where ordinary life is perfectly happy to nod and move on. Writing sees figures where life sees things; things we leave behind, figures we keep. Even the experience of numbness, when traced on paper, acquires a resigned and disenchanted grace, a melancholy cadence that seems at once intimate and aroused compared with the original blah. Write about numbness, and numbness turns into something. Upset flat surfaces, dig out their shadows, and you've got dreammaking.

Does writing, as I did later that day, seek out words the better to stir and un-numb us to life—or does writing provide surrogate pleasures the better to numb us to experience?

Three years in Rome and I had never touched this street. It would be just like me scarcely to touch anything, or to have grazed this city all but unintentionally, the way, in the three years I saw the Gypsy girl seated on her corrugated piece of cardboard next to the tramway stop, I never made a dent into her sealed, impenetrable, surly gaze. I called her the dirty girl to hide arousal and disturbance whenever I spoke of her to my friends at school.

Was I disappointed? It seemed a crime not to stumble on at least one quivering leftover from the past. Did numbness mean that even the memory of hating this street had gone away? Could parts of us just die to the past so that returning brings nothing back?

Or was I relieved? The romance of time had fallen flat. There was no past to dig up here—never had been any. I might as well never have lived here at all.

I felt like someone trying to step on his own shadow, or like a reader who failed to underline a book as a teenager and now, decades later, is totally unable to recover the young reader he'd once been.

But then, coming back from the West, perhaps it was I who was the shadow, not this street, not the books I had read here, not who I once was.

For a second, as I stood and looked at our tiny rounded balcony, I felt an urge to call myself to the window, the way Italians always shout your name from downstairs on the sidewalk and ask you to come to the window. But I wasn't calling myself. I was just trying to picture what I'd be doing behind that window so many years ago. It's past mid-July, there's no beach, no friends, I'm more or less locked up in my room, reading, and as always shielding myself from the outside world behind drawn shutters, desperately using books to put an imaginary screen between me and Via Clelia.

Anything but Via Clelia.

In that room on Via Clelia, I managed to create a world that corresponded to nothing outside it. My books, my city, myself. All I had to do then was let the novels I was reading lend their aura to this street and drop an illusory film over its buildings, a film that washed down Via Clelia like a sheet of rainwater, casting a shimmering spell on this hard, humdrum, here-and-now area of lower-middle-class Rome. On rainy days when the emptied street gleamed in the early evening, I might have been very much alone in my room upstairs, but I was alone in D. H. Lawrence's "faintly humming, glowing town"—by far the better. Dying winter light took me straightaway to the solitary embankments of Dostoyevsky's white nights in Saint Petersburg. And on sunny mornings when shouts from the marketplace a block down couldn't have sounded more truculent, I was in Baudelaire's splenetic, rain-washed Paris, and because there were echoes of Baudelaire's Paris around me, suddenly the loutish *romanaccio*, which I learned to love only after leaving Rome, began to acquire an earthy, Gallic coarseness that made it almost tolerable, vibrant, authentic. Earlier in the morning, when I opened the windows, I was suddenly in Wordsworth's England where "domes, theatres, and temples lie . . . glittering in the smokeless air" beneath the Beatles' "blue suburban skies."

And when I finally put down Lampedusa's *The Leopard* and began to see aging, patrician Sicilians everywhere, each more lost than the other in a scowling new world that none of them could begin to fathom, much less belong to, I knew I was not alone. All that these Sicilians had left was their roughshod arrogance, their ancient, beaten-down palace with its many, many rooms and rickety balconies that looked over the shoulders of history back to the Norman invasion of Sicily. One could step out onto Via Clelia and enter a tiny park where scrawny trees and scorched growth told me I'd stepped into the abandoned hunting grounds of Frederick II of Hohenstaufen.

Anything but Via Clelia.

So, why shouldn't Via Clelia feel dead now? It had never been alive. I had hated it from my very first day and had almost managed to hate Rome because of it.

And yet, as though to punish me now for calquing my own images over these sidewalks long ago, Via Clelia was giving them all back—but not a thing more. Here, Baudelaire's vendors, take them; here's Raskolnikov's hat, *you* wear it; over there, Akaky's overcoat, *yours*; and if you looked over across the Appia Nuova through Oblomov's smoky windows, you'd find Lampedusa's declining mansion, and farther out, D. H. Lawrence's town—all, all yours now. I had lined the world with books; now the city was giving them back to me, one by one, as one returns a tool, unused, or a necktie, unworn, or money that should never have been borrowed, or a book one had no intention of reading. The snow of Joyce's "The Dead," which had mantled Via Clelia after midnight one evening and given it a luster that would never have existed outside of books, was being returned to me with a curt inscription: "It never snows on Via Clelia, didn't you know?" De Quincey's London, Browning's Florence, Camus's Oran, Whitman's New York had been waiting in escrow year after mildewed year. "Truth wasn't good enough for you, was it?" asked the street, irony flecking each of its features.

The illusory film, the shadow of my three years here, was all I had. And as I walked back from one end of Via Clelia to the other with my wife and sons, I realized that all I'd be able to cull here were the fictions, the lies I'd laid down upon this street to make it habitable. Dreammaking and dissemblance, then as now.

It dawned on me much later that evening that our truest, most private moments, like our truest, most private memories, are made of just such unreal, flimsy stuff. Fictions.

Via Clelia was my street of lies. Some lies, like impacted chewing gum, were so thoroughly stepped over each day that there was no undoing or erasing them. Look at this corner, that store, this printer's shop, and all you'll see is Stendhal, Nerval, Flaubert. Underneath, nothing. Just the memory of three years waiting for our visas to the States to come through.

We had no television in those days, no money, no shopping to take our minds off anything, no friends, hardly any relatives, no point in even discussing a weekly allowance. All my mother gave me was enough money to buy one paperback a week. This I did for three years. Buying a book was simply my way of running away from Via Clelia, taking the number 85 bus on Saturdays, and spending the rest of the day burrowed in Rome's many foreign-language bookstores. The walk from one bookstore to the other without paying attention to the city itself became my way of being in Rome, of knowing Rome—a Rome that, for all my reclusive bookishness, was no less real to me than was the Rome of everyday Romans or the Rome tourists came looking for. My centers were bookshops and, between them, a network of cobbled, narrow lanes lined by ocher walls and refuse. The piazzas with their centered obelisks, the museums, the churches, the glorious remnants were for other people.

On Saturday mornings, I would get off at San Silvestro and wander downtown, hoping to get lost, because I loved nothing

better than stumbling on one of my bookstores. I grew to like the
old city: Campo Marzio, Campo de' Fiori, Piazza Rotonda. I liked
the muted affluence of rundown buildings I knew were palatial
inside. I liked them on Saturday mornings, at noon, and on weekday evenings. Via Del Babuino was my Faubourg Saint-Germain,
Via Frattina my Nevsky Prospekt, streets where people crowded
dimly lit sidewalks that could, within seconds, seem studded by
turn-of-the-century gas lamps flickering in the evening's spellbound afterglow.

I even liked the people who suddenly popped out of
seventeenth-century buildings, leading flashy, extravagant,
dream-made lives where love, movies, and fast cars took you to
places the number 85 bus knew not a thing about. I liked hanging around awhile after the bookstores had closed and the streets
had begun to empty and amble about in this magical part of the
city whose narrow cobbled lanes and spotty lights seemed to
know, long before I did, where my footsteps were aching to turn.
I began to think that over and above Via Clelia and the books I'd
come looking for, something else was keeping me from heading
back home now, and that if books had given me a destination that
was a good enough alibi for my parents and for myself, my staying in old Rome now had a different purpose. I'd grown to love
old Rome, a Rome that seemed more in me than it was out in
Rome itself, because, in this very Rome I'd grown to love, there
was perhaps more of me in it than there was of Rome, so that I
was never sure if my love was genuine or simply a product of my
own yearnings thrown at the first old lane that crossed my path.

It would take decades to realize that this strange, shadow
Rome of my own invention was everyone else's as well. Who
would have guessed . . . I'd been hiding my shamefaced, lonely-
adolescence Rome from everyone, yet all I had to do was share
one picture, and everyone, young or old, knew exactly . . . Emer-
son: "To believe that what is true for you in your private heart is

true for all men—that is genius. Speak your latent conviction, and it shall be the universal sense."

It wasn't Rome itself I was seeing; it was the film, the filter I'd placed on the old city that finally made me love it, the film I went to seek each time I'd go to a bookstore and would come out late in the evening to stroll down my Nevsky Prospekt in search of vague smiles and fellowship in a city I wasn't even sure existed on the sidewalks. It is the film I can no longer lift off the many books I read back then, the film that reverberates over time and continues to make Rome mine long after I've lost it. And perhaps it is the film I go in search of each time I'm back in Rome—not Rome. We seldom ever see, or read, or love things as they in themselves really are, nor, for that matter, do we even know our impressions of them as they really are. What matters is knowing what we see when we see other than what lies before us. It is the film we see, the film that breathes essence into otherwise lifeless objects, the film we crave to share with others. What we reach for and what ultimately touches us is the radiance we've projected on things, not the things themselves—the envelope, not the letter, the wrapping, not the gift.

Lucretius says that all objects release films, or "peeled skins" of themselves. These intimations travel from the objects and beings around us and eventually reach our senses. But the opposite is also true: we radiate films of what we have within us and project them onto everything we see—which is how we become aware of the world and, ultimately, why we come to love it. Without these films, these fictions, which are both our alibis and the archive of our innermost life, we have no way to connect to or touch anything.

I learned to read and to love books much as I learned to know and to love Rome: not only by intuiting undisclosed passageways everywhere but also by seeing more of me in books than there probably was, because everything I read seemed more in me already than on the pages themselves. I knew that my way of reading books might be aberrant, just as I knew that figuring my way around Rome as I did would shock the fussiest of tourists.

I was after something intimate and I learned to spot it in the first alley, in the first verse of a poem, on the first glance of a stranger. Great books, like great cities, always let us find things we think are only in us and couldn't possibly belong elsewhere but that turn out to be broadcast everywhere we look. Great artists are those who give us what we think was already ours. Never mind that we've never seen, felt, or lived through anything remotely similar. The artist converts us; he steals and refashions our past, and like songs from our adolescence, gives us the picture of our youth as we wished it to be back then—never as it really was. He gives us our secret wishfilm back.

Suddenly, the insights nursed by strangers belong, against all odds, to us as well. We know what an author desires, what he dissembles; we even know why. The better a writer, the better he erases his footprints—yet the better the writer, the more he wants us to intuit and put back those parts he chose to hide. With the right hunch, you could read the inflection of an author's soul on a single comma, in one sentence, and from that one sentence seize the whole book, his life work.

With the right hunch. Pascal: *"Il faut deviner, mais bien deviner."* You have to guess—but guess right.

What I found in the authors I grew to love was precisely the right to assume that I hadn't misread them at all, that I wasn't making up what I was seeing, and that I was getting the obvious meaning as well as the one they were not too keen to proclaim and might gainsay if confronted, perhaps because they themselves were not seeing it as clearly as they should, or were pretending not to. I was intuiting something for which there was no proof but that I knew was essential, because without this one unstated thing, their work wouldn't hold.

It never occurred to me then that insight and intuition, which are the essence, the genius, of all criticism, are born from this intimate fusion of self with something or someone else. To everything—books, places, people—I brought a desire to *steal into* and intuit something undisclosed, perhaps because I mistrusted all appearances, or because I was so withdrawn that I needed to believe others were as dissembled and withdrawn as I feared I was. Perhaps I loved prying. Perhaps insight was like touching—but without asking, without risk. Perhaps spying was my way of reaching out to the Roman life that was all around me. In the words of Emanuele Tesauro: "We enjoy seeing our own thoughts blossom in someone's mind, while that someone is equally pleased to spy what our own mind furtively conceals." I was a cipher. But, like me, everyone else was a cipher as well. Ultimately, I wanted to peer into books, places, and people because wherever I looked I was always looking for myself, or for traces of myself, or better yet, for a world out there filled with people and characters who could be made to be like me, because being like me and being me and liking the things I liked was nothing more than their roundabout way of being as close to, as open to, and as bound to me as I wished to be to them. The world in my image. All I cared for were streets that bore my name and the trace of my passage there; and all I wanted were novels in which everyone's soul was laid bare and *anatomized*, because nothing interested me more than the nether, undisclosed aspects of people and things that were identical to mine. Exposed, everyone would turn out to be just like me. They understood me, I understood them, we were no longer strangers. I dissembled, they dissembled. The more they were like me, the more I'd learn to accept and perhaps grow to like who I was. My hunches, my insights were nothing more than furtive ways of bridging the insuperable distance between me and the world.

In the end, my solitude, my disaffection, my shame on Via Clelia, and my wish to withdraw into an imaginary nineteenth-century bubble were not incidental to the books I was reading.

My disaffection was part of what I saw in these books and was essential to my reading of them, just as what I read in Ovid was not unrelated to my tremulous yearnings for the swarthy knees of the Gypsy girl. But they were essential in an altogether strange and undisclosed manner. I wasn't identifying with Dostoyevsky's characters because I too was poor or withdrawn, any more than I was identifying with the lusts of Byblis and of Salmacis because I would have given anything to undress the Gypsy girl in my bedroom. What my favorite authors were asking of me was that I read them intimately—not an invitation to read my own pulse on someone else's work, but to read an author's pulse as though it were my own, the height of presumption, because it presupposed that by trusting my deepest, most intimate thoughts about a book, I was in fact tapping on, or rather divining, the author's own. It was an invitation to read not what others had taught me to read, but to see what I, by virtue of the films I brought to everything, was seeing, yet to see things in such a way that the very few who heard me report what I'd seen would agree that they too had always seen things in exactly the same way. The more solipsistic and idiosyncratic my insights were, the more people said they nursed the very same ones themselves.

Maybe this is why I liked every French *roman d'analyse*. Everyone was after intimacy in those novels, yet everyone dissembled and knew that everyone else did so as well. Over and above every plot their authors spun and every grand idea they jiggled before their readers, the one thrilling moment in these novels always came when their authors bored through that amorphous landfill of inhibition called the psyche and wrote something like: *Her lover knew, by the way she showed every conceivable proof of love for him, that she was determined to say no to him.* Or: *Her future husband could tell, by the way she blushed whenever they were alone together, that she felt neither love, nor passion, nor desire for him; her blushes came from exaggerated modesty, which in her coy, girlish way she was pleased to mistake for love. The very means meant to conceal her blushes is precisely what gave them away. Her husband guessed by how happy his wife was when she heard that their friend was not going to join them on their trip to Spain that he was the one with whom she'd have betrayed him if only she had the courage. Or: The frown with which she seemed to dismiss the man she wished she didn't love told him everything he longed to know. Even the abrupt, rude manner with which she snapped at him as soon as they were alone was a good sign: she was more in love with him than he had ever hoped.*

Then, one summer evening, a sentence suddenly pops up and seems to determine the course of my life.

Je crus que si quelque chose pouvait rallumer les sentiments que vous aviez eus pour moi, c'était de vous faire voir que les miens étaient changés; mais de vous le faire voir en feignant de vous le cacher, et comme si je n'eusse pas eu la force de vous l'avouer.

[I thought that if anything could rekindle your feelings for me, it was to let you see that mine too had changed, but to let you see this by feigning to wish to conceal it from you, as if I lacked the courage to acknowledge it to you.]

This sentence was me. I reread this sentence from *La Princesse de Clèves* many times over. The letter of a woman who wins back the man who jilted her was no less intimate and dissembled than I was in my days and nights. If she succeeds in rekindling his love, it's not by feigning indifference for him—he would have seen through this feint easily enough—but merely by pretending to want to conceal a budding indifference that seizes her almost against her will. There was so much guile and so much insight in her letter that for the first time in my life I knew that what I needed to navigate the multiple removes of La Fayette's prose was nothing more than the courage to think that I had lived this sentence, that I was this sentence more than this sentence was La Fayette's.

By coincidence—and if it wasn't a coincidence, what was it?— the evening I discovered this sentence fell on a Wednesday on the number 85 bus. As I walked with my *Princesse de Clèves* on my way home, the girl at the small supermarket was sweeping the floor by the sidewalk wearing her light-blue tunic. She caught me walking by and gave me her usual ill-tempered stare. I looked away. When, fifteen minutes later, I went to redeem our bottles, she emptied the bag, lined the bottles on the glass counter as she always did, and, after dropping the coins into the change plate, leaned over toward me and, extending her right hand, elbow touching elbow, rubbed her index finger the length of my bare forearm, quietly, softly, slowly. I felt my lungs choke, as I fought the impulse to withdraw my arm, something at once spellbound and illicit racing through my chest. Her touch might have been a sibling's sympathy caress, or anything ranging from a don't-forget-your-change-now, to a let's-test-if-you're-ticklish, or a you're-sweet, I-like-you, relax!, or just simply stay-well, be-happy. Then, for the first time, and perhaps because she seemed less busy than usual, she smiled. I smiled back, diffidently, barely hearing what she said. We'd exchanged no more than four sentences.

I had wanted smiles and fellowship. And smiles and fellow-ship I'd gotten. Someone, a stranger, had read me through and through—down to my jitters, my wants, my second thoughts. She knew I knew she knew. Was it possible that I spoke the same lan-guage as everybody else?

It took weeks to screw up the courage to pass by the store

again. Trying not to look nervous, trying to seem mildly distracted as well, trying to show that I was capable of bandying a joke or two if prompted, trying to find safe ways to retreat in case she stared me down again—with all these feelings sparring in my mind, I heard her remember my name while I had all but forgotten hers.

I tried to cover up my mistake. Blushes, shortness of breath, more blushes. How paradoxical, that I, the most innocent boy on Via Clelia, should turn out to seem no better than a cad who forgets names—and should be tormented both for being so hopelessly enamored and for suggesting the very opposite. I decided to milk this newfound roguery by overdoing and showing I was overdoing my apologies, hoping she'd disbelieve them. "One of these days we should go to the movies," she said. I nodded a breathless and sheepish yes. It took me forever to realize that "one of these days" meant this very evening—last row, dark, empty weekday movie theater. "I can't," I said, trying to sound abstract, meaning never. It didn't seem to faze her at all. "Whenever you want, then."

That same Saturday evening, while coming back from bookstores downtown, I saw her standing with her beau at the bus stop across the way. They were headed downtown. They weren't even touching, but you could tell they were together. He was older. Figures. She had washed her hair and was wearing flashy, party clothes. Why wasn't I surprised? I felt rage coursing up my body, around my temples. I hated everything—the street, her, me.

I put off going to the small supermarket. With the visa approaching, part of me had left that store behind long before I stopped going there. Soon, I'd be in New York, where another me, who wasn't even born yet, might never remember any of this. By next winter when it snows there, I'd never think back on this corner.

It would never have occurred to me that this other me one day would give anything to run into the shadow me trapped under Via Clelia.

.

So on my return visit with my family, I looked for the tiny supermarket, hoping not to find it, or, rather, saving it for last. When
we reached the end of Via Clelia I realized that the store was
gone. Perhaps I'd forgotten where it was. But a second look, and
another across the street, even—as though the shop might have
shifted to the other side, or had always been across the way—told
me there was no doubt about it. It was gone. All I'd hoped was to
recapture the thrill, the fear, the thumping in my chest each time
I caught her eyes on those evenings when I'd go to redeem our
bottles. Perhaps I longed to walk back into that same store and
see for myself—my way of closing the circle, settling the score,
having the last word. I'd have walked in, leaned against the glass
counter, and just waited awhile, just waited, see what comes up,
who turns up, see if the ritual had changed, see if I'd be the same
person on the same errand on the same street.

To make light of my disappointment and draw their laughter,
I told my sons all that happened in the tiny supermarket: woman
rubbing her finger on Dad's forearm, body touching body—was
ever a come-on more explicit?—Dad running for cover under Grand-
ma's kitchen apron, and as always scampering back to his books,
never daring to go back, while skulking and prowling the streets
for days and weeks afterward—for years, I should have said—for
decades and a lifetime. "Were you in love with her?" one of my
sons finally asked. I didn't think so; love had nothing to do with
it. "So you never spoke again," said another. No, we never did.

But I hadn't told them the truth, the whole truth. I might as
well have been lying. Would they know? Would they dust for the
footprints I had erased in the hope they'd ask the right question,
knowing that, if they asked the right question, they'd have
guessed the answer already, and that if they'd guessed it, they'd
be reading my pulse as if it were their own?

Writing—as I did later that day—is intended to dig out the

fault lines where truth and dissembling shift places. Or is it meant to bury them even deeper?

Before leaving, I took one last look at Via Clelia. All those rides on the bus, the walks through Rome, the books, the faces, the waiting for visas that I sometimes wished might never come because I had grown to like this place, the vitamin shots, the conversations at the kitchen table, Gina who almost seemed to rush out in tears sometimes, and the dream launched like a desperate call on a winter night when I finished reading "The Dead" and thought to myself, I must head west and leave this town and seek a world where snow falls "softly" "into the dark mutinous Shannon waves"—all, all of it no more than a film, the aura of my love for Rome that was perhaps no more than my love for a might-be life born from a story Joyce had penned during his hapless stay in Rome, thinking of his half-real, half-remembered Dublin. The cold nights staring out my window as rain fell obliquely against the lamplight; the evening I came so close to another body that I knew I could no longer live like this; the sense that life could have started or just turned on this improbable three-block stretch—all of it a film, perhaps the best and most enduring part of me, but a film all the same. All I'd encountered here were half-truths. Rome, a half-truth, Via Clelia, a half-truth, the adolescent who ran errands after school, his books, the Gypsy girl, the girl from the supermarket, half-truths as well, even my return trip now, a muddle of half-truths veiling the numbing thought that, if I never really wanted to come back here and had been putting it off for years, it was also because, much as I thought I hated it, I wished I'd never left at all.

Did I know what this numbness was? I blamed it on my fictions, my films, my impulse to deflect the here and now by proposing elsewheres and otherwises. But perhaps numbness had a more troubling side. And as I neared the Furio Camillo Metro station and could no longer see Via Clelia, something did begin to come to me, distantly at first, then, as we were about to enter

the station, with a fierceness I'd never expected: Via Clelia was
not just littered with the many books I'd read there, but what it
harbored unchanged, untouched after forty years, were chilling
premonitions of the city across the Atlantic for which I knew
I'd have to abandon Rome some day soon, a city that terrified
me and which I hadn't seen yet and feared I might never learn to
fathom, much less love. That city had been dogging me during
my three years in Rome. I'd have to learn to like another city all
over again—wouldn't I?—learn to put new books on the face of yet
another place, learn to unlove this one, learn to forget, learn not
to look back, learn new habits, learn a new idiom, learn a new me
all over again. I remember exactly the spot where this discovery
had filled me with disquieting premonitions: in a used bookstore
on Via Camilla where I'd found by pure chance a tattered old
copy of *Miss Lonelyhearts* and simply hated it, hated the thought
of moving to a country where people liked and read such books.
And on that spot it had finally dawned on me that, if I had never
wanted to live in Rome, still I would have given everything to
stay here, on this street, with these people, with their language,
their yelps, their seedy movie theaters, the girl from the supermarket, and eventually become as surly and kindhearted as each
and every one of them had been to me.

Outside of that bookstore the uncanny questions had bub-
bled up before I could quell them: What was Rome without me?
What would happen to Rome once I no longer lived there? Would
it go on without me, Baudelaire, Lawrence, Lampedusa, and
Joyce? One might as well ask what happens to life when we're no
longer there to live it.

I was like someone who comes back to life after being dead
and finds traces everywhere of how naïvely he'd imagined death.
For a moment, it was as if I had never been to America at all yet,
as if all those years away from Rome had never happened. But I
also felt like someone who comes back to life and has no recol-

lection of death. I didn't know whether I was here or there. I knew nothing. The pitch-dark center of hell is a cloud of unknowing where words are tongue-tied and where writing, as I discovered that evening, is useless. I'd settled absolutely nothing, and the work that remained to be done here hadn't even started, might never start, was never meant to be.

I had been preparing myself for this return trip, even before leaving Rome. In those days it was going to be a permanent return. "This thing with America," I'd imagined myself saying, "never really worked." Being back would not hurt nor would it surprise me. By rehearsing failure in America, I had made my return to Rome seem easier, unavoidable, imminent, which in its turn made leaving for America seem a fantasy, an unnecessary whim almost, something that might never happen, could never happen, had yet to happen in an unreal and distant future that suddenly became less scary because I had found so many ways to deny it was ever going to happen.

Now I was back to a place I had never really left.

Correction: I was back to a place I was never coming back to again. Or if I were to one day, I'd come back on the number 85 bus—alone. And remember, among other things, coming here with my family. I told my wife and sons I was happy they had come with me. I told them it was good to come back, good to be heading back soon, good they didn't let me come back alone. But I spoke these words without conviction, and would have thought I hadn't meant them had I not grown used to the notion that speaking without conviction is how I speak the truth. What roundabouts, though, for what others feel so easily. Roundabout love, roundabout intimacy, roundabout truths. In this, at least, I had stayed the same.

My Monet Moment

The romance begins for me with a picture of a house by Claude Monet on my wall calendar. More than half the house is missing and the roof is entirely cropped. All one can see is an arched balcony with hints of another balcony on the floor above. Outside, wild growth and fronds everywhere, a few slim trees—palms mostly, but one agave plant stands out—and beyond, along a wide, unpaved road, four large villas and a dappled sky. Farther out in the distance is a chain of mountains capped with what could be snow. My instincts tell me there is a beach nearby.

I like not knowing anything about the house or the painting. I like speculating about the setting and imagining that it could easily be France, Italy, possibly elsewhere. I like thinking that I'm right about the wide expanse of seawater behind the house. I stare at the picture and fantasize about the torpor hanging over old beach towns on early July days, when the squares and roads are empty and everyone stays out of the sun.

The caption, when I finally cheat and find it at the bottom of the calendar, reads "Villas in Bordighera." I've never heard of Bordighera before. Where is it? Near Lake Como? In Morocco? On Corfu? Somewhere in Asia Minor? I like not knowing. Knowing anything about the painting would most likely undo its spell. But I can't help myself, and soon I look up more things, and sure enough, Bordighera, I discover, lies on the water, on the Riviera

di Ponente in Italy, within sight of Monaco. Further research reveals the villa's architect: Charles Garnier, famed for building
the Opéra de Paris. Finally, the year of the painting: 1884. Monet,
I realize, was still a few years away from painting his thirty-plus
views of Rouen Cathedral.

I know I'm bit by bit demystifying the house. As it turns out,
the Internet reveals more paintings of gardens and palm trees in
Bordighera, plus one of the very same house. It is a copy of the image on my wall calendar, painted by Monet, not in Bordighera but
later that same year in Giverny and meant as a gift for his friend
the painter Berthe Morisot. The second painting, *Strada Romana*,
depicts an identical view of the same unpaved road with villas farther off but with one exception: the large house built by Garnier is
altogether missing. Monet might be playing at omitting the house
only to have it resurface in another painting, trying the scene "now
with," "now without" the house. Monet might be interested in neither the house nor the road. All he cares about is the lull that settles on the Mediterranean around noontide and that he is not even
sure he's not making it up. Which is also why he needs to paint it.
If it's there, he's captured it; if it isn't, well, it's there now. What he
is looking to capture may be a shape, an arrangement of colors, a
pattern, a rhythm, a perspective, an instantaneity, as he called it,
or just the transit of light, which Monet frequently complains
changes no sooner he attempts to paint it. It spells the difference
between impressions of morning and noon.

Monet went to visit Bordighera for the light. His intended visit of
a couple of weeks ended up lasting three laborious months in the
winter of 1884. He had come the previous year with the painter
Renoir for a brief stay. This time he was determined to come alone
and capture Bordighera's seascapes and lush vegetation. His letters were filled with accounts of his struggles to paint Bordighera.

They were also littered with references to the colony of British residents who flocked here from fall to early spring each year and who transformed this fishing and agrarian sea town famed for its lemons and olive presses into an enchanted turn-of-the-century station for the privileged and happy few. The Brits ended up building a private library, an Anglican church, and Italy's first tennis courts, to say nothing of grand luxury hotels, precursors of those yet to be built on the Venice Lido. Monet felt adrift in Bordighera. He missed his home in Giverny and Alice Hoschedé, his mistress and later wife; and he missed their children.

As far as he was concerned, Bordighera promised three things: Francesco Moreno's estate, containing one of Europe's most exotic botanical gardens; breathtaking sea vistas; and that one unavoidable belfry with its dimpled, onion cupola towering over everything. Monet couldn't touch one of these without invoking the other two. Lush vegetation, seascapes, towering belfry—he kept coming back to them, painting them separately or together, shifting them around as a photographer would members of a family who were not cooperating for a group portrait.

If he was forever complaining, it may have been because the subject matter was near impossible to capture on canvas, or because the colors were, as Monet liked to say in his letters, terribly difficult—he felt at once entranced, challenged, and stymied by them. But it was also because Monet was less interested in subject matter and colors than he was in the atmosphere and in the intangible and, as he called it, the "fairylike" quality of Bordighera. "The motif is of secondary importance to me," he wrote elsewhere. "What I want to reproduce is what lies between the subject and me." What he was after hangs between the visible and the invisible, between the here and now and the seemingly elsewhere. Earth, light, water are a clutter of endless, meaningless things; art is about discovery and design and a reasoning with chaos.

In the end, perhaps, what Monet liked best of all was the ritual of painting, and what he wanted to capture was not just Bordighera but the ritual of painting Bordighera, perhaps in memory of the first time he'd seen Bordighera and had thought of painting it, or of the second, when he finally came with his easel and brushes, or of the third, when he realized that he liked painting this town more than he loved the town itself, because what he loved was more in him than in the town itself, though he needed the town to draw it out of him.

Many years after seeing the reproduction on my wall calendar, I finally happen upon Monet's third painting of that very same house at an exhibition in the Wildenstein gallery in New York. Same missing back of the house, same vegetation, same sky, same suggestion of a beach just steps away, except that the third floor, which is absent in the first two canvases, is quite visible here; one can almost spot the balusters lining the balcony. And there is another variation: in the background looms not the snowcapped mountains but Bordighera Alta—the *città alta*, the oldest part of the city—which like so many old towns in Italy is perched on top of a hill and predates the *borgo marino* on the shore. This inversion is also typical of Monet. He wanted to see how the scene looked from the other side.

I want to be in that house, own that house. I begin to people it with imaginary faces. A plotline suggests itself, the beach beckons ever more fiercely. Like a fleeing cartoon character painting escape routes on a wall, I find my own way into this villa and am already picturing dull routines that come with ownership.

Then one day, by chance, I finally find the opportunity to visit Bordighera and to see it for myself. I have to give a talk on Lake

Como, so rather than fly directly from New York to Milan I decide to fly to Nice instead and there board a train to Italy. The bus from the airport to the train station in Nice takes twenty minutes, purchasing the train ticket another fifteen, and as luck would have it, the train to Italy leaves in another fifteen. Within an hour I am in Bordighera. The train stops. I hear voices on the platform. The door opens and I step down. This is exactly what I expected. Part of me is reluctant to accept that art and reality can make such good partners.

I don't want a taxi, I want to linger, I want to walk to my hotel. Before me, leading straight from the small train station and cutting its way through the heart of the town, is a palm-lined avenue called the Corso Italia, once known as the Via Regina Elena. I've arrived, as I always knew I would, in the very early afternoon. The town is quiet, the light dazzling, the turquoise sea intensely placid. This is my Monet moment.

I've come to Bordighera for Monet, not Bordighera—the way some go to Nice to see what Matisse saw, or to Arles and Saint-Rémy to see the world through the eyes of van Gogh. I've come for something I know doesn't exist. For artists seldom teach us to see better. They teach us to see other than what's there to be seen. I want to see Bordighera with Monet's eyes. I want to see both what lies before me and what else he saw that wasn't quite there, and which hovers over his paintings like the ghost of an unremembered landscape. Monet was probably drawing from something that was more in him than out here in Bordighera, but whose inflection we recognize as though it's always been in us as well. In art we do not see, we recognize. Monet needed Bordighera to help him see something he'd spot the moment he captured it, not before; we need Monet to recognize what we've long sought but know we've never seen.

My first stop, I tell myself, will be the house on the Via Romana, my second the belfry, and my third the Moreno gardens. Luckily, my hotel is on the Via Romana too.

As I walk, I cannot believe what I am seeing: plants and trees everywhere. The scents are powerful and the air pure, clean, tropical. Right before me is a mandarin tree. Something tells me the potted lemons are false. I reach out through a fence and touch them. They are real. A huge late-nineteenth-century building, surrounded by tall palm trees, sits on a hill where the Corso Italia runs into the Via Romana. I should have booked a room there instead. It turns out that what was once a grand hotel in the posh Victorian style is now the front entrance of an emergency room. This demotion annoys me; but the restoration work is impeccable, and the façade bears the lingering resonance of bygone times.

I force myself to think positively of the hotel I booked online. I even like the silence that greets me as I arrive and step up to the front desk. Upstairs, I am happy to find I have a good room, with a good-enough balcony view of the distant water, though the space between the hotel and the sea is totally obstructed by a litter of tiny brick houses of recent vintage. I take out clean clothes, shower, and, camera in hand, head downstairs to ask the attendant where I can find the Moreno gardens. The man at the desk looks puzzled and says he's never heard of the Moreno gardens. He steps into the back office and comes out accompanied by a woman who is probably the proprietress. She has never heard of the Moreno gardens either.

My second question, regarding the house painted by Monet, brings me no closer to the truth. Neither has heard of such a house. The house is on the Via Romana, I say. Once again, the two exchange bewildered looks. As far as they know, none of the houses here were painted by Monet.

Monet's Bordighera is gone, and with it, most likely, the house by the sea. On the Via Romana, I stop someone and ask if she could point me in the direction of the town's belfry. Belfry? There is no belfry. My heart sinks. Minutes later I run into an older gentleman and ask him the same question. Shaking his head, the man apologizes; he was born and raised here but knows of no campanile. I feel like a Kafkaesque tourist asking average Alexandrians where the ancient lighthouse stands, not realizing that nothing remains of the ancient Greek city.

Yet, as I'm walking, suddenly something interesting appears within sight. It's a huge building, yet another one of those immense hotels in the grand style. I'm sure they'll know about the campanile, and Villa Moreno, and about Monet's villa.

But the huge hotel building, which has Thomas Mann written all over it, is not only totally locked up but also in a shambles. The grounds have gone totally feral. The building is in tatters, its walls peeling, the windows broken in; even the windows are either gaping holes or their wooden planks are sagging and about to fall off. Those windows that have retained their old weather-beaten shutters are in no less parlous a state of decay; the balconies look as though they are ready to teeter, and their ancient banisters are reduced to a wasted filigree of rust so thin and flaky that they'd crack if you so much as brushed them with your pinky. One wonders what fowl and wild cats run free inside. Appropriately enough, the name of this large establishment is Villa Angst, once a luxury hotel, built and owned by a Swiss man.

Everything I look at here seems suddenly touched by the ghost of a beckoning past. This, it occurs to me, is not even a ruin. A ruin is a building that has died and stopped decaying. This one is crumbling still, has a few more years to go before extinction, still tussles with the specter of bitterness and shame on its ramshackle features. I don't want to find Monet's house if this is what has happened to it.

I walk away. The words *Hotel Angst* resonate ominously, though I am totally unable to fathom the meaning of the encounter. I have come looking for the source of art and find decrepitude instead. Everywhere I look now has suddenly acquired an

air of irredeemable decay; I stare at Bordighera through a film that
is no longer Monet's; it's my film, my mirror, my cipher now—
perhaps my narrative all along. I feel like someone visiting the
land of his ancestors for the first time. He knows better than to
expect the spirit of lost forebears to rise up and lead him back to
the old homestead. But he still hopes to connect to something.
What he finds instead is wreckage and phantom lanes and a
locked gate to a defunctive world.

From the Via Romana, I make my way back to the train station,
where earlier I had spotted a few restaurants on the long seaside
promenade called Lungomare Argentina, probably because Eva
Perón loved it. Yet along the way—and I barely have time to realize it—there it is: the belfry I've been searching for. It looks exactly as in Monet's paintings, with its glistening, mottled, enamel
rococo cupola. The name of the church is Chiesa dell'Immacolata
Concezione, built by none other than Charles Garnier. It's probably the tallest structure in town. How could anyone not know
what I was referring to when I kept asking about a campanile? I
snap pictures, more pictures, trying to make the photos look like
Monets, exactly as I did twenty minutes earlier when I stumbled
upon a public garden with leafy dwarf palms that resemble those
Monet painted in Moreno's garden. An old lady who stops and
stares at me suggests that I visit the *città alta*, the town's historic
center. It's not too far from here, she says, impossible to miss if
I keep bearing left.

Half an hour later, I'm on the verge of giving up on the *città
alta* when something else suddenly comes into view: a small hill
town and, towering above it, another belfry with a bulbous cupola
almost identical to the one I spotted on the *chiesa* by the shore. I
can't believe my luck. Bordighera, I realize, has not one but two
steeples. The steeple in Monet's paintings is not necessarily that of

Garnier's church by the marina but probably another one that I didn't even know existed. Coastal towns always needed towers to warn of approaching pirate ships; Bordighera was no exception. A steep, paved walkway flanked by old buildings opens before me; I'll put off my visit to the historic center and walk up to the top of this minuscule town instead. But this, it takes me yet another delayed moment to realize, is the *città alta* I came looking for. My entire journey, it appears, is made of uninformed double takes and inadvertent steps.

Bordighera Alta is a fortified, pentagon-shaped medieval town full of narrow, seemingly circuitous alleys whose buildings are frequently buttressed by arches running from one side of an alley to the other, sometimes creating vaulted structures linking both sides. Laundry hangs from so many windows that you can scarcely see the sky from below. The town is exceptionally clean—the gutters have been covered with stones, and the clay-tiled paving is tastefully inconspicuous. Except for a televised news report emanating from more than one window lining the narrow Via Dritta, everything here is emphatically quiet for so packed a warren of homes. As I make my way around the square, I see the Santa Maria Maddalena's clock tower again, and to my complete surprise, once I step into a large courtyard that might as well be a square behind the main square, another belfry comes into view. Then a post office. A church. A barber. A baker. A high-end but tiny restaurant, a bar, an *enoteca*, all tucked away serendipitously so as not to intrude on this ancient but glitzified town. A few local boys are playing *calcetto*, or pickup soccer. Others are chatting and leaning against a wall, all smoking. A girl, also smoking, is sitting on a scooter. I can't decide whether this town is inhabited by working-class people stuck on this small hill all year or whether the whole place has been refurbished to look faux-run-down and posh-medieval. Either way, I could live here, summer and winter, forever.

Once again, through an unforeseen ascent of a hill, I've stumbled upon something perhaps far better than what I came looking for. I find myself suspecting that the humbling, intrusive hand of Providence is arranging events which couldn't seem more random. I like the idea of a design behind my desultory wanderings around Bordighera. I like thinking that perhaps this is how we should always travel, without foresight or answers, adventitiously, with faith as our compass.

As I'm making my way through a maze of narrow lanes, I finally come to an open spot that looks out toward a huge expanse of aquamarine. Straight below me is a marina. I decide to head back down to the Lungomare Argentina and am beginning to leave Bordighera Alta. Because I am already planning my return trip to Bordighera in six months, I stop at what looks like a picturesque two-star hotel. I walk inside and start by asking the man at the desk for the price of a double. Then, as though my next question follows up on the previous one, I ask if he can tell me something about the Moreno gardens. Once again I am given the same story. There are no Moreno gardens. "But Monet—" I am about to interrupt. "Moreno's land was broken up more than a century ago," says a portly man who had been chatting with the hotel's owner and was sitting in the shade. Francesco Moreno, he continues, came from Marseille and, like his father before him, was a French consul in Italy—he owned almost all of Bordighera and was in the olive and the lemon trade. He imported all manner of plants from around the world, which is why Monet tried everything he could to be allowed inside the garden. The estate, however, was sacrificed to build the Via Romana.

Moreno, it appears, did not put up a fight with the city planners, even though he was the wealthiest landowner in sight. He died, probably a broken man, in 1885, one year after Monet's visit. The family sold their land, gave the rest away, then his widow moved to Marseille. The Morenos never returned. There is scarcely a trace of the Moreno mansion or its grounds—or, for that matter, the Moreno family. For some reason no one wants to talk about them—the way no one talks about Herr Angst either.

It's only then, as I leave the hotel and take a steep path to the church of Sant'Ampelio by the sea, that I finally spot a white house that might very well be the house, or something that looks just like it, though I could, of course, be wrong. A rush of excitement tells me that I have found it all on my own—yes, adventitiously. Still, I could be wrong. It is a gleaming white construction; Monet's house is not so white nor does it have a turret. But then, I've only seen cropped versions of it. I walk down the path and head right to the house. There is no doubt: same balconies, same stack of floors, same balusters. I approach the villa with my usual misgivings, fearing dogs or a mean guardian or, worse yet, being wrong.

I brace myself and ring the buzzer by the metal gate. "Who is it?" asks a woman's voice. I tell her that I am a visitor from New York who would give anything to see the house. "*Attenda*, wait," she interrupts. Before I can compose an appropriately beseeching tone in my voice, I hear a buzzer and the click of the electric latch being released. I step inside. A glass door to the house opens and out steps a nun.

She must have heard my story a thousand times. "Would you like to see the house?" The question baffles me. I would love to, I say, still trying to muster earnest apology in my voice. She asks me to follow and leads me into the house. She shows me the office, then the living room, then what she calls the television room, where three old women are sitting in the dark watching the news. Is this a nunnery? Or a nursing home? I don't dare ask. She shows me into the pantry, where today's menu is written in large blue script. I can't resist snapping a picture. She giggles as she watches me fiddle with my camera, then shows me to the dining room, which is the most serene, sunlit dining room I have seen in ages.

It is furnished with separate tables that could easily seat thirty people; they must be the happiest thirty I know. The room is impeccably restored to look its age, its century-old paintings and heavy curtains bunched against the lintel of each French window. The house must cost a fortune in upkeep.

Would I like to take a look at the rooms upstairs? asks the nun. Seriously? She apologizes that her legs don't always permit her to go up and down the stairway but tells me I should feel free to go upstairs and look around, and must not forget to unlock the door leading to the top floor on the turret. The view, she says, is stupendous. We speak about Monet. She does not think Monet ever stepped inside this villa, but he must have spent many, many hours outside.

I walk up the stairs gingerly, amazed by the cleanliness of the shining wooden staircase. I admire the newly corniced wallpaper on each floor. The banister itself is buffed smooth, and the doors are a glistening enamel white. What timeless peace these people must live in. When I arrive at the top floor, I know I am about to step into a view I never thought existed, and will never forget. And yet there I was, minutes earlier, persuaded that the house was turned to rubble or that they weren't going to let me in. I unlock the wooden door. I am finally on the veranda, staring at the very same balusters I saw in Monet's painting in the New York gallery, and all around me is . . . the sea, the world, infinity itself. Inside the turret is a coiling metal staircase that leads to the summit. I cannot resist. I have found the house, I have seen the house, I am in the house. This is where running, where searching, where stumbling, where everything stops. I try to imagine the balcony a hundred years ago and the house a century from now. I am speechless.

Later, I come down and find the nun in the kitchen with a Filipina helper. Together, the nun and I stroll into the exotic garden. She points to a place somewhere in the far distance. "There are days when you can see the very tip of Monte Carlo from here. But today is not a good day. It might rain," she says, indicating gathering clouds.

Is this place a museum? I finally ask. No, she replies, a hotel, run by Josephine nuns. A hotel for anyone? I ask, suspecting a catch somewhere. Yes, anyone.

She leads me back into an office where she pulls out a brochure and a price sheet. "We charge thirty-five euros a day." I ask what the name of this hotel is. She looks at me, stupefied. "Villa Garnier!" she says, as if to imply, what else could it possibly be called? Garnier built it, he died here, and so did his beloved son. The widow Garnier, unlike Moreno's, stayed in Bordighera.

It would be just like me to travel all the way to Bordighera from the United States and never once look up the current name of the villa. Any art book could have told me that its name was Villa Garnier. Anyone at the station could have pointed immediately to it had I asked for it by name. I would have spared myself hours of meandering about town. But then, unlike Ulysses, I would have arrived straight to Ithaca and never once encountered Circe or Calypso, never met Nausicaa or heard the enchanting strains of the Sirens' song, never gotten sufficiently lost to experience the sudden, disconcerting moment of arriving in, of all places, the right place. What luck, though, to have found Villa Angst and the belfries and heard the sad tale of the Moreno household, or to have walked into an art gallery in New York one day and seen the other version of a painting that had become like home to me, and if not home, then the idea of home—which is good enough. I tell her I'll come back to the Villa Garnier in six months.

But the nun has one more surprise in store for me.

Since I've come this far for Monet, she suggests, I should head out to a school on the Via Romana that is run by other nuns and is called the Villa Palmizi, for the palm trees growing on what was once Moreno grounds. The school, which is totally restored, she tells me, contains part of the old manor house.

We say goodbye and I head out to the Villa Palmizi, eager to speak to one of the nuns there. The walk takes five minutes. The end of one search has suddenly given rise to another. I knock, a nun opens. I tell her why I've come. She listens to what I have to say about Monet, about the Villa Garnier, then asks me to wait. Another nun materializes and takes her place. Then another. Yes, says the third, pointing to one end of the house that has recently been restored, this was part of the Moreno house. She says she'll take me upstairs.

More climbing. Most of the schoolchildren have already gone home. Some are still waiting for their parents, who are late picking them up. Same as in New York, I say. We climb one more flight and end up in a large laundry room where one nun is ironing clothes while another folds towels. Come, come, she signals, as if to say, Don't be shy. She opens a door and we step onto the roof terrace. Once again, I am struck by one of the most magnificent vistas I have ever seen. "Monet used to come to paint here as a guest of Signor Moreno." I instantly recognize the scene from art books and begin to snap pictures. Then the nun corrects herself. "Actually, he used to paint from up there," she says, pointing to another floor I hadn't noticed that is perched right above the roof. *"Questo è l'oblò di Monet."* "This is Monet's porthole." I want to climb the narrow staircase to see what Monet saw from that very porthole. "This," she points out to a giant tree, "is the tallest pine tree in Europe." It was probably already in place when Monet sat here. All I can think of is the words of Giovanni Ruffini, the novelist most responsible for turning Bordighera into the English hot spot it became after the publication of his novel *Doctor Antonio* in 1861: "from the pale gray olive to the dark-foliaged cypress." This is where it started.

The story of Monet's *oblò* is most likely apocryphal, but I need to see what Monet might have seen through this oblong window just as I needed to come to Bordighera to see the house for myself. A sense of finality hovers in my coming up here to see the town through Monet's window. Same belfry, same sea, same swaying palms, all staring back now as they did for Monet more than a century ago.

I begin to nurse an eddy of feelings that cannot possibly exist together: intense gratitude for having witnessed so much when I was so ready to give up, coupled with the unsettling disappointment which comes from knowing that, but for luck and my own carelessness, I would never have witnessed any of this, and that, because luck played so great a part in things today, whatever I am able to garner from this experience is bound to fade. Part of me wishes to make sense of all this, only to realize in a flash of insight as I'm standing in Monet's room, that if chance—what the Greeks called Tyche—trumps meaning and sense every time, then art, or what they called Techne, is itself nothing more than an attempt to give a tone, a cadence, a meaning to what might otherwise be left to chance.

All I want to do, all I can do is retrace my steps and play the journey over again. Stumble on the image of a house on my wall calendar, spot the same house in a gallery, arrive by train, know nothing, see nothing, never sight the old *città alta* until I come upon it, see the town "with" and "without" the belfry, with and without the sea, with and without Villa Angst, or the chopped-up quarter of Moreno's house, and always, always chance upon Garnier's home last. I want to restore this moment, I want to take this moment back with me.

Stepping out of Monet's tiny room, I am convinced more than ever that I have found what I came looking for. Not just the house or the town or the shoreline but Monet's eyes to the world, Monet's hold on the world, Monet's gift to the world.

Temporizing

Following the disastrous defeats of Roman troops at Lake Trasimene and Cannae—the bloodiest in ancient history—the Roman general, consul, and dictator Quintus Fabius Maximus Verrucosus came up with a brilliant strategy to contend with Hannibal's superior forces. He would not confront the enemy; he would simply delay engaging the Carthaginians, all the while dogging them in the hope of wearing them down. The strategy proved successful, ultimately making possible Scipio's bolder move, which put an end to the Second Punic War with the invasion of Carthage. For this Fabius earned the name *cunctator*, meaning delayer, from which English derives the noun *cunctation*. Until this very day, Fabius Maximus is known in most schoolbooks as the *temporizer*, the delayer—the more usual translation of *cunctator*—which means: he who waits out his enemy, who makes time, who, to use a more current and pedestrian term, gives the enemy time. It is also the first thing I learned when I was taught angling as a boy. Let your prey think he's safe, draw him in, cut him slack, lure him until you've got him well and tight, then . . . yank as hard as you can. It is ironic that the victim of this strategy should himself have floundered because of it: *Hannibal ante portas*. Hannibal stops before the gates of Rome and puts off certain victory until . . . another time.

To "give time" is also a strategy by which the person put in an inferior position tries to contend with a superior force. You would never temporize with a weakling; you pummel a weakling, but you tire out a giant. Here the endangered and threatened temporizer "waits his time," "bides his time," "plays for time," "gains time," "marks time." To temporize means to do what is necessary to tide you over until a more favorable time comes. To temporize means to step out of time's continuum, to put time on hold, to stop time from happening, to open an epochal space. You find a dimple in time and you burrow and hide in it and let real time—or what others call real time—slide by you. You are, as one is with modern watches, operating on two, perhaps more, time zones.

A temporizer procrastinates. He forfeits the present. He moves elsewhere in time. He moves from the present to the future, from the past to the present, from the present to the past, or, as I've already suggested in my essay "Arbitrage," in *False Papers*, he "firms up the present by experiencing it from the future as a moment in the past."

I come to the verb *to temporize* in two ways, and both are indissolubly fused to my life as a scholar of the seventeenth century and as a memoirist of our times. The third is a direct extrapolation of the first two.

First of all, I immediately latched onto the word because, as one says of the children of Holocaust survivors, I am a child of temporizers. I was born in Egypt in a Jewish family whose members saw the writing on the wall but decided to wait out their foes. Don't do anything rash, put off risking what you have for what you may never get, above all lie low—all these are the mantras of congenital temporizers. They reflect a fear of acting typical of those who are either temperamentally or materially conditioned to prefer speculating rather than acting. It's the ruse of the possum: if you do nothing, and danger sees you doing nothing, danger will go away. Ultimately, what it really says is this: if I kill myself a tiny bit each day before you do, won't this obviate your need for killing me? If I stop my watch, won't history stop its own?

Like a submarine that wants to appear hit, you leave a slick behind you. It may cost you, but everyone knows that what you leave for others to see is not really vital; it is the slough you molted, the carapace, dead tissue, sepia, decoy stuff. Time, however, has gone into hibernation—or, in the case of crustaceans, in estivation. Live tissue, live time is happening elsewhere.

That I am a descendant of Marranos, who temporized in Spain at the time of the Inquisition, invokes the second meaning of the word. This time I came across it in, among others, Carlo Ginzburg's book on Nicodemism. Originally, I had looked into Nicodemism because I was interested in the Counter-Reformation and its manifold handbooks on the art of prudence and was pleased to discover that Christians too practiced their own variegated brands of Marranism. Among the books quoted by Professor Ginzburg was one published in England, which I also found in the *OED* as a citation from 1555: "The Temporisour (that is to say: the Observer of Tyme, or he that changeth with Tyme)." Which suggests the other meaning of temporizing. To temporize not only means to wait out something but also to compromise, to parley, to delay taking a position; it means to waver, to adapt, to conform, to evade, to shift, to fudge, to trim. Temporizing is what you do when you don't want to act, or when you can't act, or when you don't know how to act, or when you are forced to act (or speak) in ways that are not your own; you become evasive, deceptive. You trim. A trimmer is a timeserver, which reminds me of George Savile's brilliant *Character of a Trimmer* in the seventeenth century. A timeserver temporizes. A timeserver is a double-dealer, a two-timer. A timeserver serves two masters. A timeserver trims with time. The suggestion of deception is inscribed in the very verb itself. As all sixteenth- and seventeenth-century moralists knew so well, from Torquato Accetto in Italy, to Baltasar Gracián in Spain, to Daniel Dyke in England (whose book was widely read in La Rochefoucauld's circle), a temporizer was in essence a hypocrite, an opportunist. A temporizer, like a trimmer, a schemer, or an equivocator, is one who puts his true feelings, thoughts, religion, or true identity aside while a storm is raging. If you cannot step elsewhere, you go under, you turn the coat.

It would take no great stretch of the imagination to draw intimate parallels between the two meanings of "temporizing" and apply them in the most superficial manner to my life. In Egypt, my family could easily see the storm brewing and hoped to wait it out, as Jews have always done throughout history; but like the Marranos in Spain, to win time, members of my family decided to convert to Christianity; others stopped going to temple. Unable or unwilling to leave, they too went under.

I am tempted to call Marranism temporizing because what I want to lay bare here is not so much the unavoidable connection between the two but what one could tentatively call a "Marranism of time." A Marrano, after all, is someone who practices two faiths simultaneously: one in secret, another in the open. Similarly, an exile is a person who is always in one place but elsewhere as well. An ironist is someone who says one thing but means another. A hypocrite is someone who upholds one thing but practices another. An arbitrageur is someone who buys in one market and sells in another. A temporizer is someone who exists in two time zones but who, for this very reason, does not exist in either. He has stepped out of time. The temporizer lives like others, with others, perhaps better than others—except that, like the Marranos in Spanish churches or like me in Egypt saluting the Egyptian flag every morning at school knowing it represented anti-Semitism in its foulest, the temporizer lets time happen without being part of it. He is not touched—or hurt—by time. He lives in abeyance.

Now, temporizing may be a historical necessity and of interest to intellectual historians, even to those interested in the fate of the Jews of the Middle East, but it is not what I'm really after. What I am trying to explore is not the historical temporizer but, for want of a better term, the psychological temporizer—who defers, denies, disperses the present, who accesses time (life, if you wish) so obliquely and in such roundabout ways and gives the present so provisional and tenuous a status that the present, insofar as such a thing is conceivable, ceases to exist, or, to be more accurate, does not count. It is unavailable. He is out of sync with it. By abstracting himself from the present, by downgrading it, what he gets in exchange is an illusory promise of security away from pain, sorrow, danger, loss. He forfeits the present because it's not what he wants it to be, because he may not know what to do with it, because he wants something else, because he is working or holding out for something better. In effect, he wants to alter, reorganize, and reconfigure his own life and, by so doing, forestall those things he fears most.

This is what one does when one burrows in a cork-lined room all day for days, for months, for years, reinventing a life for oneself. By so doing, one renounces time, transcends time, etherealizes time. For all he knows, such a person, such a writer, may have been fending off the present all his life, so that a retelling of that life, however altered the account may be, constitutes not only a temporizing act—it will keep the author so busy that he won't be able to leave his room—but in itself is also a narrative about a psychological temporizer. Proust's novel is about a man who looks back to a time when all he did was look forward to better times. To rephrase this somewhat: he looks back to a time when what he looked forward to was perhaps nothing more than sitting down and writing . . . and therefore looking back.

What gives meaning to a life so clearly inscribed in temporizing is not someone's ability to confront pain, sorrow, or loss, but rather someone's *ability to craft ways around pain, sorrow, loss*. It is the craft that makes life meaningful, not the life itself. This, clearly, is a bookish concern and a bookish solution. Yet it is only by removing life from the present, or from what Proust called the *tyrannie du particulier*, from the tyranny of day-to-day, hard-and-fast, here-and-now, nuts-and-bolts facts, that by a sort of detour the temporizer will access time and experience. What stands between him and life is not his fear of the present; it is the present. I could mention Proust again but it is the poet Leopardi who comes most vividly to mind: his moments of true happiness were not in "lived" life. That was never given to him, since Leopardi's life was, as he saw it, a tissue of undiminished sorrows. It was in remembering these selfsame sorrows, or rather in crafting elaborate ways back to them, that Leopardi the poet came upon his only source of joy.

Temporizing, in this context, is not just a strategy for material or psychological survival in a world perceived as hostile but also becomes a form of consciousness. And by consciousness I don't even mean what kind of good or bad conscience do temporizers have, or how can one go on being who one is and at the same time temporize and be, as the saying goes, "not altogether there." Rather, the question I would like to address—and, here, let me broach the third "way" to which I alluded earlier: *Is temporizing an aesthetic move? Can one speak of an aesthetics of temporizing?* A temporizer may very well be a hypocrite with a good conscience or a sincere man with a bad one; his face and the mask he wears are not identical, or his face could very well be the only mask he or others will ever see. Either way, a temporizer has a consciousness of being other, of not being in sync with who he is or with who others think he is. He is other than who he is because his "timing" is not like everyone else's.

Everything about him is shifty. The place he calls home could easily stop being his, just as his possessions could easily be taken away. Those he loves are other than who he thinks they are, and what people swear to seldom holds over time. One could push this description further: the temporizer even treats those closest to him already as people whom he will unavoidably lose. To buffer the blow, which he knows must come, he rehearses and steels himself to their loss while they're still very much in his life. He looks at his grandmother and sees the dead woman she is likely to be soon; he looks at his mistress and already sees his "sweet cheat gone." He is taking a distance that life itself has by no means made necessary. He is mourning someone who is still alive, the way he'll find ways to feel jealous of someone he has long since ceased to love. He regrets what he hasn't lost or, for that matter, isn't even in possession of to worry he might lose it one day.

I am, of course, thinking of Proust. And yet this is the irony with Proust. Marcel always wishes he could have anticipated losing someone; for then, he thinks, he would have suffered less. Similarly, he always wishes his mind could catch up with his wishes when they're about to be realized, for then, so he thinks, he would maximize his pleasure. These, however, are merely strategies for managing the unmanageable intensity of the present, for rehearsing, for "scripting" the present. Caught unprepared, Proust's protagonist is either totally disabled or totally devastated. When Albertine is finally willing to offer herself to Marcel, Marcel prefers to take a rain check instead. When Marcel has finally overcome what seemed like mild grief over his grandmother's death, he is suddenly caught by a spasm so violent as he bends down to tie his shoelaces that he bursts out crying.

Everything in Proust's universe aims to prevent similar outpourings. His temporizing antics aim to diffuse experience, to make experience unavailable, to thwart experience in the real world unless it has first passed through what one could call a literary time filter. His whole life is spent crafting that filter. One can see this even in his sentences: they are prototypically crafted to do one thing best of all: to temporize. They throw their net ever wider, waiting, never rushing, prodding, teasing, coaxing, luring, angling, as if something far greater, but whose character or profile the author still ignores and is certainly not about to disturb or risk losing by reaching too soon for it, is waiting for him at the end of the line at some hitherto unknown point in the future that, once we get to it, will—as is so typical of the span of each of Proust's sentences—"shed a retrospective illumination" upon his entire work.

Despite Proust's shrewd and fretful comings and goings from one time zone to the other, Marcel, the character, is never prepared *in time.* He is always surprised by the unexpected, as though Proust were always reminding himself that no matter how cautiously Marcel shields himself and defers contact with the cruel world, the way Oedipus tried to avert his own fate, that world has an insidious way of slipping back in. Proust has made being clumsy or getting caught off guard—call it the Proustian slip—a veritable art form, a privileged moment indeed, because it is only inadvertently, by slipping, that Marcel encounters the present and, as he himself knows, life itself, with its pleasures, its dangers, and sorrows. And yet, the one thing Marcel wishes desperately to learn to do is precisely how to filter pleasure from its attendant dangers and sorrows. He should learn how to distrust more, take his distance, never be so hasty or so zealous in wanting things now and only now. The lesson he should learn is simple enough—and he's made it an art form as well: *what is* should always be turned into a *what seems*; *what seems* must become *what isn't*; and *what isn't, what was.* This is how things acquire meaning—not vis-à-vis the real present, but before the higher court of something I'd like to call the imperfect-conditional-anterior-preterit: *what was perhaps and might have been* has more meaning than *what just is.* This is where Proust wishes to lodge all experience, and this is where *la vraie vie* occurs. Memory and wishful thinking are filters through which he registers, processes, and understands present experience. With temporizers, experience is meaningless—it is not even experience—unless it comes as the memory of experience, or, which amounts to the same, as the memory of unrealized experience. For Proust, it is only retrospectively, long after the present has slipped away, that one finally sees the bigger picture. It is only when it's too late that one comes to understand how close one came to bliss ... or how needless our sorrows were when they drove us to despair. The following is by Emily Dickinson:

> *Except the Heaven had come so near—*
> *So seemed to choose My Door—*
> *The Distance would not haunt me so—*
> *I had not hoped—before—*
>
> *But just to hear the Grace depart—*
> *I never thought to see—*
> *Afflicts me with a Double loss—*
> *'Tis lost—And lost to me—*

Proust's job is to throw experience back into the past and from there—let me use a verb I introduced earlier—yank it back from the future, *retro-prospectively*. This is what gives that unmistakable span, that spread to his sentences. In that spread, past and future and, by implication, present exist at the same exact time.

Temporizing comes to the present the long way around, the way some people come to love, counterintuitively. Some seize today on condition they'll come back to it tomorrow. Some reach out for what life throws their way provided they come close enough to almost lose it. And some elegize the past, knowing that what they truly love is not the past they've lost or the things they elegize and learn to think they love but their ability to speak their love for it, a love that may never have even been there but which is none other than the child of their ability to craft their way into some sort of imperfect-conditional-anterior-preterit. Writing, they seem to say, works. Writing will get you there. Burrowing in a cork-lined room reinventing your life is life, is the present.

And when you have doubts, simply saying how frail is your hold on the present can become a gratifying act. Therein lies the true aesthetic of temporizing: by admitting, by showing that we do not know how to live in the present and may never learn to do so, or how thoroughly unsuited and unprepared we are to live our own lives, we do not necessarily make up for this inability. But we uncover a hitherto unsuspected surrogate pleasure: in making the realization of this unsuitability become a redemptive testimonial. Playing with the disconnect between all the possibilities implicit in the imperfect-conditional-anterior-preterit may be a highly dysfunctional move, and is only destined to backfire each time, but it also gives us our life back as . . . fiction.

Indeed, the disconnect, the hiatus, the tiny synapse—call it once again the spread between us and time, between who we are and wish we might have been—is all we have to understand our place in life. One measures time not in units of experience but in increments of hope and anticipated regret.

One reason I think I make a terrible travel journalist is that, as soon as I visit a place, I am totally unable to write about it. Not that I need to let things "simmer down" (as we say) but that I need to feel that such-and-such a place has lost its presence, that it has become unavailable, or that I might never see it again. I am walking its streets and yet, for the purposes of the article I have been sent to write and have promised to submit as soon as I return to the United States, I must pretend I am no longer on these very same streets. If I want to write I must pretend to remember. Writing outside of loss leaves me at a loss . . .

In a sentence from *Out of Egypt* I describe the sound of my deaf mother's shriek, saying that it reminded me of the screech of tires coming to a sudden halt. Big tires. Bus tires.

> This, [my father] would find out one day, was the howl of
> the deaf, when the deaf are in pain, when the deaf quar-

rel, when they scream, when words fail them and nothing comes out but this sputter of shrieks that sounded more like a fleet of busses screeching to a halt on a quiet beach-day Sunday than like the voice of the woman he had married.

The part I would like to focus on for a second is not the yell itself but the "quiet beach-day Sunday" with which it is contrasted. Translators never get it right because it is untranslatable, because in principle it doesn't even exist or make sense: what is a "quiet beach-day Sunday"?

And yet if those quiet beach-day Sundays mean anything to me today and if, as so many Alexandrians have written to me after reading *Out of Egypt*, the idea of a quiet moment on Sundays just before crowds begin to head out to the beaches captures the very essence of life in Alexandria in very late spring or early summer, when summer beaches have not quite become the congested bedlam they invariably turn into by July but still retain the promise of magic to come in the weeks ahead—if all this means anything to me today, it is because it has far less to do with Alexandria than it does with how I've imposed Egypt on my present life in America. For this impression of a quiet beach-day Sunday was born not in Egypt, but in America one morning when I was walking with my father on Riverside Drive during our first year here and, seeing a group of twenty-year-olds sunbathing on a grassy incline off Ninety-eighth Street, turned to him and said, "This is a beach-day, isn't it?"

I devoted about twenty pages of *Out of Egypt* to the description of an early Sunday morning at the beach. Then I closed that segment by relating how I frequently remembered these beach mornings with a friend in graduate school in Cambridge many years later. This memory, however, was born in New York City, was then shipped to Cambridge, then brought back to New York,

where, many years later still, I eventually wrote *Out of Egypt*
and, by so doing, finally dispatched this entire *entassement* and
imbrication of cities to an imagined Alexandria.

Egypt is just the grid, the matrix, the cavity into which I
"throw back" my life long after leaving Egypt. My present is
meaningless unless it is *thrown back* to Egypt. One could say that
all of my impressions of Egypt are no more than scattered pieces
of my life out of Egypt strung together and *thrown back* into a
narrative thread I've decided to call Egypt. Seeing Egypt, not
America, is how I see America. I see the present provided it's like
the past, becomes the past. When I went back to visit Egypt after
publishing *Out of Egypt*, all I could think of, or kept trying to
think of, was New York—a place that used to loom like a distant
future for me when I was a boy but that had suddenly become my
present only when I wasn't present in it! Egypt, however, the Egypt
I had for so many decades dreamed of, was not once before me.

My impulse when I see something beautiful or moving or
even something I desire in the here and now is to throw it back to
Egypt, to see if it fits back there, if it isn't yet another one of those
myriad missing pieces that belongs there or that should be brought
back there, or that should be made to seem to have originated
there, as though for something to make sense to me it has to have
roots that go all the way back to Egypt, as though the act of piec-
ing Egypt back together, of reconstructing and restoring even an
imaginary Egypt out of this scatter of impressions in New York
were an interminable restoration project whose purpose is to prevent all contact with the present, so that anything I encounter that
strikes me must, in one way or another, correspond to something
Egyptian, have an Egyptian coefficient, or else mean absolutely
nothing. Things that do not have an Egyptian analog do not register, have no narrative. Things that happen in the present without echoing even an imaginary past do not register either. They
cease to exist. They do not count. There are interminable stretches

of New York that do not exist for me: they don't have Egypt, they have no past, they mean nothing. Unless I can forge an Egyptian fiction around them, if only as a mood I recognize as Egyptian, they are as dead to me as I am dead to them.

Egypt is my catalyst; I break down life in Egyptian units, the way archaeologists cut up the temple of Dendur in numbered blocks to be put together . . . anywhere else.

Perhaps it was to ease the feeling of loneliness and estrangement on Riverside Drive that morning with my father that I imagined a similar scene on the beaches of Alexandria during that magical Sunday hour in the morning.

I so envied these people on the grassy incline who probably lived close to the park and who kept bringing iced tea from their homes in the surrounding prewar buildings, who knew who they were, and who they were likely to become, and who seemed so thoroughly grounded in the present. I wanted nothing more than to be lifted from where I stood and be one of them, leave my time scheme and join theirs. Instead, I took these people on the grassy incline and brought them back with me to my imaginary Egypt, made them my friends, and drank cold lemonade with them on the beaches of my teens and with them walked along the sand dunes, and to drive the point home, I even had one of them turn to me and say, as I'd told my father that day, "This is a perfect beach-day morning, isn't it?"

Ultimately, what I remembered while writing *Out of Egypt* was not our life at the beach but the fiction I had invented that day of our life at the beach.

Indeed, the parts of *Out of Egypt* that matter to me the most are not those set in Egypt but those where the solitary, awkward, inadequate narrator goes looking in Europe and America for the remains of Egypt. He yearns for Egypt, but he doesn't even yearn for it the way those who enjoyed life in Egypt sometimes miss Egypt. They almost never long for the past; they deride the very

notion of remembrances of things past. They've always been an-
chored in life, in the things of the here and now, and now that
they are elsewhere, this is where they claim and have staked
their lives. The narrator of *Out of Egypt*, on the other hand, has
a liquid and unsteady foothold. It is not even Egypt or the things
he remembers that he loves; what he loves is just remembering,
because remembering ensures that the present won't ever prevail.
Remembering is merely a posture that turns its head away and,
in the process, even when there is nothing to remember, is shrewd
enough to make up memories—surrogate, standby memories—if
only to justify not having to look straight at the present.

Alexandria, as Lawrence Durrell once wrote, may very well be
the capital of memory. But Alexandria wouldn't exist if memory
hadn't invented it.

Reflections of an
Uncertain Jew

The man in this 1921 photograph is sixty-five years old, bald, with what looks like a white trimmed beard, his left hand poised not so much on his left waist as on his lower left hip, displacing the side of his jacket, his bearing confident, a bit menacing perhaps, and yet, despite the purposeful and intentionally secure posture, always a touch apprehensive. As with all the older men in my father's family album, in his hand, which is slightly uplifted, he is holding something that looks like a cigarillo, though it is somewhat thicker than a cigarillo, but not quite as big as a cigar; at its tip there seem to be ashes. One might say (if only to mimic a famous reconstructive analysis of how Michelangelo's Moses holds his tablets) that it is almost as though the photographer had not warned his subject in time, and therefore the subject, thinking this was a pause in between takes, went for a quick puff and didn't manage to remove the guilty cigarillo in time, so that the cigarillo, from being an item to be kept out of the picture, once caught, ends up occupying center stage.

Something tells me, however, it might just as easily be a small pen instead. Still, one doesn't hold a pen between one's middle and index fingers, especially with the hand turned outward in so relaxed a manner. No, not a pen. Besides, why would a pen appear when the subject is standing up and when there clearly is no desk anywhere in the background? It must be a cigar.

On closer inspection, it seems that there is something quite studied in his relaxed posture: one hand akimbo, the other almost placing the cigarette on exhibit, not as an afterthought, not diffidently, but declaratively. The ashes themselves say quite a bit: they are not about to spill, as may have seemed at first; they are in fact honed to a point, as with a pencil sharpener, which is why I thought of a pen, a ballpoint, all the while knowing that ballpoints did not exist at the time this picture was taken. Stranger yet, there is no smoke emanating from the cigarillo, which suggests either that the smoke was touched up and blotted out in the photo lab, or that the cigarillo was never even lit.

Which means that the cigarillo in the photo has a totally intentional presence.

What is this gentleman—and there is no doubt, since the posture proves he is a gentleman—doing exhibiting his cigarillo that way? Could it be that this is just a cigarillo, or is it much more than a cigarillo, much more than a pen, even, the ur-symbol of all symbols, not just of defiance, of menace, of security, or of wrath, even, but simply of power? This man knows who he is; despite his age, he is strong, and he can prove it; witness his cigarillo—it doesn't spill its ashes.

Another, younger picture of the same subject, taken around 1905, suggests more or less the same thing. The hair is neatly combed—there is much more of it—the beard, though grayish, is bushier. Behind the seated subject is a reproduction of Michelangelo's statue of a dying slave, standing in naked and contorted agony. The man in this photograph stares at the camera with something like a very mild stoop, his shoulders less confident, uneasy, almost cramped. He looks tired, overworked, worn out; in his left hand he is holding a cigar that seems to have been smoked all the way down; he is holding its puny remains at one or two centimeters above the spot where his thighs meet, almost—and I stress the *almost*—echoing the flaunted nudity of the dying slave behind him.

I may have made too much of the symbolism here. I would, let me hasten to say, respectfully withdraw every word, were it not for the fact that the subject of these two pictures, ostensibly fraught with Freudian symbolism, is none other than Freud himself. How can anyone look at Freud's cigarillo and not think Freudian thoughts?

However, there is another symbol at work here. Indeed, looking back at the pictures, it occurs to me that something had clearly happened between the older man standing up in 1922 and the somewhat younger man sitting down in 1905. What happened, of course, is success.

The man in the later picture is an established man. A man of property, of substance. His is the pose that all men adopted when being photographed: it conveyed composure, worldliness, confidence, plenitude, security, a touch of arrogance perhaps, but without a doubt, this was a man of the world, a much-traveled, sought-after individual who had seen and lived much. In fact he was more than just established, he had made it, he had, as the French say, arrived. An *arriviste* is someone who strives to arrive; a *parvenu*, however, is someone who has arrived. You posed with a cigarette, or a cigar, or a cigarillo, not just because the cigar suggested security—as though those with, as opposed to without, cigars were worthier men—but also because the cigarillo was an instrument, an implement, a prosthesis for grounding oneself in the picture and, by extension, in the world. Smoking doesn't suggest success, it screams success. It locks it in. A successful Jew who smokes is living proof that he has attained a degree of prominence.

Let me resort to another word, which is much used nowadays and which conveys a neo-Jewish nightmare: this man had assimilated. *Assimilate* is a strange verb, used without a direct or indirect object to mean being swallowed up, absorbed, and incorporated into mainstream Gentile society. But the verb has another meaning, closely linked to its etymology: *to assimilate* means to become similar to, to simulate.

The irony is that this was how one posed to simulate success. You were photographed with a smoking implement to appear you weren't posing, to appear as though you had achieved enough stature not to have to pose at all. You posed with a cigar to suggest you weren't posing with a cigar. You belonged and, therefore, no longer had to worry about belonging. The Italians may have called this posturing *sprezzatura*; add a pipe and the complications reach Magrittian proportions. A Jew poses with a cigar to symbolize two things: that he has achieved social and professional success, but also that he has successfully assimilated.

There were many other Jews with cigars.

There is a picture of a plump, extremely groomed, self-satisfied young gentleman wearing clothes that were clearly cut by the best tailor. He is seated with one arm resting on a thigh, and another holding out a cigarillo more or less in the manner of Freud; his face looks up smugly, with a rakish glint on his smile. His name is Artur Schnabel.

Another is caught walking along the street holding his pipe in his hand. He is wearing an unbecoming wide-brimmed hat. He could not look more gawkish or more self-conscious. He is feigning a debonair amble about town, but he is holding a pipe no less gingerly than if he were walking a urine sample to a laboratory. His name is Albert Einstein.

Another is not even looking at the camera, his hand supporting his chin while grasping a cigarette. He looks like the most established intellectual, and yet if there is a man who has come to symbolize the most unestablished intellectual of this century it is precisely Walter Benjamin, who died on the run.

There is also a picture of a young woman, perhaps one of the boldest intellectuals of her times, looking totally intimidated and fainthearted, having enlisted the help of this implement for the picture, and yet holding her cigarette at bay, almost pushing it out of the picture (the way some New York cabbies do when they hold

their cigarettes out of the window), all the while desperately cling-
ing to it, hoping it might give her that certain air without which
she'd be a simple undergraduate. Her name is Hannah Arendt.

Finally, there is the picture of the greatest Italian novelist of
this century, the man who first introduced Freud to Italy and who
indeed translated Freud, and who took on a name that is itself
quite interesting: Italo Svevo, also known as the man who made
compulsive smoking a subject worthy of modern literature. He is
sitting with legs crossed, holding a cigar over one thigh in a gesture that could be called Freudian.

Freud, Schnabel, Einstein, Benjamin, Arendt, Svevo—*didn't
they know?*

Didn't they know that smoking, besides giving you cancer,
confers no power, no composure, no confidence whatsoever?

But this is not the question I meant to ask. This was just my
way of dissembling the real question, as though I too had something to dissemble and needed to mislead the reader somewhat
before coming out with it, as though by raising the smokescreen
of Freudian symbolism I could sneak in another, more disquieting question, which reflects my own very personal worries and
anxieties, not Freud's or Einstein's.

Didn't they know they were Jewish?

Or, to turn it around: Didn't they know that, even if all Europe posed this way, it would never wash, that they could never
pass, that part of what made them so odious to anti-Semites was
the very fact that they presumed they could pass? Didn't they know
that, while others posed with a cigar to suggest they weren't posing
with a cigar, such a pose, when it came to Jews, was a double pose
and as such came close to a form of imposture that brought out
the killer in every anti-Semite?

What was so threatening to a German, to an Austrian, to a
Frenchman or an Englishman in this cigar posture was not just that
Jews had made it into mainstream German, Austrian, French, or

British society. What was really threatening about such Jews was that they were also the very first to have accessed pan-European culture. In fact, they didn't just tap into such a culture; they built it.

They were enamored of cosmopolitan European civilization not only because, unlike national venues, it flung open far wider doors to them, but also because, all the while not being properly speaking theirs, it was more theirs than any other nation's. Their romance with the Christian or pagan culture was irresistible precisely because it allowed them to draw much closer than they had ever been to those cultures that only a few generations before had been barred to them. Moreover, it allowed them to realize that being Jewish did not mean they couldn't get at the center of the Christian universe and understand it, perhaps, even better than did Christians. Benjamin's unfinished doctoral dissertation was on the theater of the post-Reformation; he was one of the very few modern thinkers to appreciate the genius of Paolo Sarpi, the sixteenth- and seventeenth-century Venetian friar who remains today the most lucid historian of the Council of Trent. Hannah Arendt wrote her dissertation on Saint Augustine under Karl Jaspers, the existential Christian philosopher. Freud, a font of encyclopedic knowledge, was fascinated by classical antiquity. And Ettore Schmitz, who changed his name to Italo Svevo to reflect both his Italian and Swabian roots, had intentionally or inadvertently forgotten to make up a third name to reflect his Jewish origins.

The list goes on and on. For cosmopolitan Jews, traditional Judaism and the traditional rewards of Judaism could not compete with the advantages and rewards of this profound and vertiginously rich European culture—could not compete, that is, with Berlin, Vienna, Paris, Rome, Milan, Trieste, London.

The city where my great-uncles posed with cigars or cigarettes between their fingers was a long way from those European cultural capitals. And yet if the world of Alexandria had one wish—and that wish lasted for seventy-five years—it was precisely to be like Berlin, Vienna, Paris, Rome, Milan, and London, to be Berlin, Vienna, Paris, Rome, Milan, and London all in one. I won't repeat the clichés; everyone knows them: Alexandria was a city where all the religions and nationalities of the world were represented, and where each religion lived side by side with the others in perfect harmony. Perfect harmony may be an exaggeration, of course, but I mean it no less facetiously than when it is said of married couples living side by side in perfect harmony. Such cosmopolitanism can exist in two ways: as it does in New York or as it did in Alexandria, i.e., in a democracy or in an empire.

In New York, there is a system of social values and beliefs that prescribes mutual toleration and equal opportunities. Prescribed does not mean practiced, but it is there on the books at least, and most people try hard enough to believe it works that they would fight for it if it were taken away from them.

In Alexandria, there were no shared values or shared beliefs. Alexandria was the product of two or even three empires: the Ottoman, the French, and the British. Empires generate their own kinds of capital cities: nerve centers where all their far-flung populations send emissaries and migrants. You go to exploit multiplicity, not to lose your identity or to respect the other more than is necessary to conduct business. You embrace multiplicity because it ratifies your identity. You learn everyone's language; and if you never lose yours to a dominant language, you do adopt a lingua franca that eventually confers an identity all its own.

Many of the people I grew up with were children of immigrant and low-end colonialist communities: Italian, Syrian, Lebanese, and French. Many of these continued to maintain contact with their country or community of origin much in the way ancient Greek colonies did: the colony of the colony of a colony frequently continued to claim ties to the mother community, say, of Athens, Thebes, or Corinth.

But then you also had a different kind of population, of which
I can recall three: the Armenians, some of whom had settled after
the first Armenian massacre; the Greeks from Asia Minor, who had
come before but who certainly thronged to Alexandria following
their exodus from Turkey and the burning of Smyrna; and then
the Jews, many of whom had been in Egypt for a thousand years,
while others arrived from elsewhere—in my family's case, from
Turkey—in an attempt to found a new home. Armenians, Greeks,
and Jews did better than the French or the Italians not only because they were more numerous but also because they were more
desperate: for them there was really no country to return to.

In this interim oasis they created their own peculiar dynamic,
acquiring paper citizenships that were to real nationalities what
paper profits are to real money. They thrived in this ideal pan-
opolis, though, as with immigrants elsewhere in the world, no
one really expected to stay there permanently. No one identified
with Alexandria, and everyone was too busy identifying with the
entire culture of Europe to understand what having a single culture really meant.

The more westernized the Jews of Alexandria grew, the more
they developed the sensibility of their German, French, and Italian Jewish counterparts: they too allowed their Jewish identity to
be displaced, not by a national identity—which was almost entirely imaginary—but by a pan-European, equally imaginary one.
We imagined every other city in the world in order not to see the
one city we were very much a part of, the way we imagined every
other culture in order to avoid seeing we were basically and just
Jewish. Some of us could afford to go through all these antic
moves because we knew—and feared—that, all things considered,
the one thing that would never be taken away from us was precisely our Jewishness. And yet, was Jewishness something at the
core, securely lodged, or was it something that had been dis-
lodged and was now spinning forever out of orbit?

Although most Jews did practice Judaism in Egypt and were

proud of being Jewish, I was always torn. I was proud of being Jewish, but I could just as easily have been mortified by being Jewish. I wanted to be Christian, but I didn't want to be anything but Jewish. I am a provisional, uncertain Jew. I am a Jew who loves Judaism provided it's on the opposite shore, provided others practice it and leave me to pursue assimilation, which I woo with the assiduity of a suitor who is determined to remain a bachelor. I am a Jew who longs to be in a world where everyone is Jewish, where I can finally let down my guard; but I am a Jew who has spent so much time defining himself in relation to non-Jews that I wouldn't know how to live, much less who to be, in a world where everyone was Jewish.

I still don't know whether the pan-Europe I dreamed up truly existed or whether it was after all a Jewish invention, a Jewish fantasy. But it may explain my single-minded devotion to European Christian and pagan literature. These books were the first I read during my youth, and it was to these books that I finally turned when I sought to locate the imaginary Europe I had totally lost on landing in Europe after Egypt.

For if anything seemed parochial and provincial and closed-minded when I landed in Europe, it was precisely Europe itself. And more provincial still was America. Yet it was in America that I finally realized that the most provincial place in the world was Alexandria, and that perhaps the ability to spot provincialism in people and places was itself the surest sign of a provincial person: i.e., someone who longs for the great and tiny tokens of cosmopolitanism for fear of being sucked back into the dark alleys of dark small towns in the dark old country that every Jew carries inside him. We needed our books, our many languages, our broadmindedness, our ability to disclaim who we were in the interest of adaptability, our fast cars and our tiny cigars, even our willingness to show we could easily live with the most disquieting paradoxes—we needed them because they were a cover for something we no longer knew how to be: Jewish.

As I write of all these paradoxes, it occurs to me that I am being cosmopolitan in a very Alexandrian way, in the way the Book of Ecclesiastes is a very Alexandrian book, because, in the beginning as in the end, to be a cosmopolitan in Alexandria was to live with every conceivable contradiction. But when it comes to the deeper, thinking self, it takes no great effort to see that without paradox I am out of place, I am a stranger, and that this very paradox, for a cosmopolitan Jew living in Alexandria, is home.

But let us not overromanticize either. What paradox does when it becomes a way of life is to alienate one, to make one a stranger from one's people, one's homeland, one's second and third homeland, and ultimately from who one is.

You become nothing, *nobody*, like Ulysses.

And Ulysses posing with a cigar is like a lotus eater who thinks he's found a new home.

So let me return to Freud's cigar and suggest—and I do so with all the hesitation in the world, because I do hate this sort of thing—that the cigar I've been toying with throughout is a phallic symbol.

But as Nietzsche said, I am giving you the moral before giving you the tale.

So let me propose an example.

It is taken from my own experience as the only Jewish boy in a 97-percent-Muslim school in Egypt (the other 3 or so percent were Christians). We are about to take swimming lessons and I complain to the teacher that I am feeling sick—and for all I know at that moment, I must be sick, because fear will do this to you. The reason is not hard to imagine. I didn't want to undress before the other boys because if I did so I'd reveal to the Catholics who thought I was Catholic, to the Greek Orthodox who always suspected I was one of theirs, or to the Muslims who assumed I was soon to convert to their religion, since I was the only European boy who attended Islam class every week, that I was—to all of them—a sham. You may not feel Jewish, but Judaism is—pardon the metaphor—cut into you, as though to make sure that, however you quibble over your Jewish identity, you are branded with it for life. You—and others—would never have a doubt. But as every Elizabethan and Jacobean playwright knew, that's precisely the tragedy of impostors. Even when they are totally alone they no longer know where their truth lies. And their awareness of this paradox resolves nothing at all.

But when I explained to some of my relatives why I hated swimming class—I who loved the sea and who loved the beach enough to wish to spend my entire life in the water, because if I am ambivalent about all things, I am certainly the most amphibian man alive—they responded with a totally different tale. During the Armenian massacre, when a Jew was mistaken for an Armenian by the Turks, all he had to do was pull down his trousers and he was given his life back.

So let me be totally blunt now and ask questions whose purpose is really not so much to arrive at answers but to give a sense of how confused I, the writer from cosmopolitan Alexandria, am on this question of the Jewish identity in a cosmopolitan world. To this end, let us assume for a split second that Freud is in fact holding a phallic symbol in his hand.

What is he saying about that phallus? Is he holding out a Jewish member and saying, "Look, ladies and gentlemen, I may be a totally cosmopolitan man, but I can never—nor do I ever wish to—forget I am Jewish"?

Or is he saying the exact opposite? "Look, stare, and observe: here is proof I am not and have never been Jewish."

Or, "Would I even allow you to raise the question if I thought you'd come up with this?"

Or is he saying something totally different? That is: "This is just a cigar. And only a Jew from Alexandria who has never understood Freud or confronted his own anxieties about being Jewish

would think otherwise. This, sir, says more about you than it ever
will about me."

And without hesitating a second I'd say that he was right,
that it is all about me and my own reluctant Judaism, which desperately wishes to find similarly reluctant Jews around the world,
if only to nurse the illusion that there are other Jews like me, that
Jews like me are not alone, that perhaps all Jews are like me, in
the sense that all Jews are other, lonely Jews, that no Jew can ever
be authentically Jewish once he steps out of the ghetto, that all
Jews have the diaspora branded on them so profoundly that feigning they are not Jewish is perhaps the surest way for them to discover they are nothing but Jewish, and that, in this strange new
world that reminds them they are free now, some part of them is
forever skulking in the dark dying to scream to another Jew: *Ceci
n'est pas un cigare.*

A Literary Pilgrim
Progresses to the Past

What my dentist cried out one day after finally removing an un-suspected fourth nerve from one of my molars comes to mind each time I try to understand myself as a writer. Do I, as a writer, have what he called a "hidden nerve"?

Don't all writers have a hidden nerve, call it a secret cham-ber, something irreducibly theirs, which stirs their prose and makes it tick and turn this way or that, and identifies them, like a signature, though it lurks far deeper than their style, or their voice or other telltale antics?

A hidden nerve is what every writer is ultimately about. It's what all writers wish to uncover when writing about themselves in this age of the personal memoir. And yet it's also the first thing every writer learns to sidestep, to disguise, as though this nerve were a deep and shameful secret that needs to be swathed in many sheaths. Some don't even know they've screened this nerve from their own gaze, let alone another's. Some crudely mistake confes-sion for introspection. Others, more cunning perhaps, open tempt-ing shortcuts and roundabout passageways, the better to mislead everyone. Some can't tell whether they're writing to strip or hide that secret nerve.

I have no idea to which category I belong.

As for a sheath, however, I'd spot mine in a second. It is place. I begin my inward journey by writing about place. Some do so by writing about love, war, suffering, cruelty, power, God, or country. I write about place, or the memory of place. I write about a city called Alexandria, which I'm supposed to have loved, and about other cities that remind me of a vanished world to which I allegedly wish to return. I write about exile, remembrance, and the passage of time. I write—so it would seem—to recapture, to preserve and return to the past, though I might just as easily be writing to forget and put that past behind me.

And yet my hidden nerve lies quite elsewhere. To work my way closer to it, I'd have to write about loss and feeling unhinged in provisional places where everyone else seems to have a home and a place, and where everyone knows what he wants, who he is, and who he's likely to become.

My Alexandrians, however, have an unsteady foothold wherever they stand; they shift time zones, life passions, loyalties, and accents with the unwieldy sense that the real world swims before them, that they are strangers in it, that they're never quite entitled to it. Yet peel this second sheath, and you'll find another.

I may write about place and displacement, but what I'm really writing about is dispersion, evasion, ambivalence: not so much a subject as a move in everything I write. I may write about little parks in New York that remind me of Rome and about tiny squares in Paris that remind me of New York, and about so many spots in the world that will ultimately take me back to Alexandria. But this crisscrossed trajectory is simply my way of showing how scattered and divided I am about everything else in life.

I may never mention dispersion or evasion by name. But I write around them. I write away from them. I write from them, the way some people write around loneliness, guilt, shame, failure, disloyalty, the better to avoid staring at them.

Ambivalence and dispersion run so deep that I don't know whether I like the place I've chosen to call my home, any more than I know whether I like the writer or even the person I am when no one's looking. And yet the very act of writing has become my way of finding a space and of building a home for myself, my way of taking a shapeless, marshy world and firming it up with paper, the way the Venetians firm up eroded land by driving wooden piles into it.

I write to give my life a form, a narrative, a chronology; and, for good measure, I seal loose ends with cadenced prose and add glitter where I know things were quite lusterless. I write to reach out to the real world, though I know that I write to stay away from a world that is still too real and never as provisional or ambivalent as I'd like it to be. In the end it's no longer, and perhaps never was, the world that I like, but writing about it. I write to find out who I am; I write to give myself the slip. I write because I am always at one remove from the world but have grown to like saying so.

Thus I turn to Alexandria, the mythical home of paradox. But Alexandria is merely an alibi, a mold, a construct. Writing about Alexandria helps me give a geographical frame to a psychological mess. Alexandria is the nickname I give this mess. Ask me to be intimate, and I'll automatically start writing about Alexandria.

I'll write about *diaspora* and *dispossession*, but these big words hold my inner tale together, the way lies help keep the truth afloat. I use the word *exile*, not because I think it is the right term, but because it approximates something far more intimate, more painful, more awkward: exile from myself, in the sense that I could so easily have had another life, lived elsewhere, loved others, been someone else.

If I keep writing about places, it is because some of them are coded ways of writing about myself: like me, they are always somewhat dated, isolated, uncertain, thrust precariously in the middle of larger cities, places that have become not just stand-ins for Alexandria, but stand-ins for me. I walk past them and think of me.

Let me turn the clock back by a few decades.

It is October 1968, and I've just arrived in New York City. Mornings are nippy. It's my second week here. I have found a job in the mailroom at Lincoln Center. During my rounds at 10:30 every morning the plaza is totally empty and its fountain silent. Here every day I am always reminded of my very early childhood, when my mother would take me for long walks along a quiet plantation road far beyond our home.

There is something serene and peaceful in this memory. I go out every morning knowing that as soon as I get a whiff of a nippy Manhattan breeze, I'll encounter the memory of those plantation mornings and the hand that held mine along these long walks.

Fast-forward more than two decades. It is 1992. On certain warm summer days at noon I go to pick up my mother on Sixtieth Street, where she still works as an office clerk. We buy fruit and sandwiches on Broadway and walk awhile until we find a shady stone bench at Lincoln Center's Damrosch Park. At times I bring my two-year-old son, who'll scamper about, eating a spoonful, then run back to hide in between raised flower beds.

Afterward, he and I walk my mother back to her office; we say goodbye, then head toward Broadway to catch the bus across from a tiny park where Dante's statue stands. I tell him of Paolo and Francesca, and of cruel Gianciotto, and of Farinata the exile and Count Ugolino who starved with his children.

Dante's statue still reminds me of the tales I told my son then; it reminds me of this park and of other small parks I've since written about, and of how I felt guilty as a son, letting my mother hold so menial a job in her seventies, taking her out for a walk when it was clearly too warm for her, and how, to write a memoir about our life in Egypt, I had hired a full-time babysitter who was only too glad to have the time off whenever I'd take my son to lunches that I resented sometimes because they'd steal me from my desk. I think back to that summer and to my explosive snubs whenever my mother complained I'd arrived too late again.

One day, after losing my temper and making her cry at lunch, I went home and wrote about how she would sit on our balcony in Alexandria smoking a cigarette, and of how the wind had fanned her hair on the day she came to pick me up at school after someone had called home saying I had been suspended that day. Together we rode the tram downtown, naming the stations one by one.

Now, whenever I look back to those hot afternoons at Lincoln Center, I see two boys, me and my son, and I see my mother both as she was during those summer lunches in the early nineties and as I remembered her on our walks along the plantation road two and a half decades earlier. But the one mother most clearly limned on those stone benches at Damrosch Park is the one riding the tram with me: serene, ebullient, carefree, catching the light of the sun on her face as she recited the name of the stations to me.

I did not lie about the names of the tram stations, but I did make up the scene about her coming to school that day. It doesn't matter. For this scene's hidden nerve lay somewhere else: in my wanting to stay home and write, in not knowing which mother I was writing about, in wishing she could be young once more, or that I might be her young boy again, or that both of us might still be in Egypt, or that we should be grateful we weren't.

Perhaps it had something to do with my failure to rescue her from work that day, which I'd inverted into her rescuing me from school; or perhaps with my reluctance to believe that an entirely invented scene could have so cathartic an effect, and that lies do purge the mind of mnemonic dead weight.

I don't know. Perhaps writing opens up a parallel universe into which, one by one, we'll move all our dearest memories and rearrange them as we please.

Perhaps this is why all memoirists lie. We alter the truth on paper so as to alter it in fact; we lie about our past and invent surrogate memories the better to make sense of our lives and live the life we know was truly ours. We write about our life, not to see it as it was but to see it as we wish others might see it, so we may borrow their gaze and begin to see our life through their eyes, not ours.

Only then, perhaps, would we begin to understand our life story, or to tolerate it and ultimately, perhaps, to find it beautiful; not that any life is ever beautiful, but the measure of a beautiful life is perhaps one that sees its blemishes, knows they can't be forgiven, and, for all that, learns each day to look the other way.

The Contrafactual Traveler

Other than money and means of transportation, the one thing a traveler needs is curiosity. You need to want to see, hear, and experience things, either for the first time or for the nth time. Those sights, that river, this or that small town, those strange ways of doing things that people in distant places have, this restaurant, that tongue, even the thrill of going to far-flung islands to shut one's eyes and zonk out on placid foreign beaches—without curiosity you wouldn't seek any of them out. True, one travels either for business or pleasure. But even the most hardened dealmaker will occasionally lift his eyes from his limousine with tinted windows, catch a glimpse of the Colosseum at midday, and say, "What I wouldn't give to slip through those arches on such a beautiful spring day." That same night he wanders down the narrow lanes of Trastevere, trying to catch a legendary whiff of Rome. As for those who travel for pleasure, the answer couldn't be more obvious: the very expectation of pleasure feeds on curiosity.

What people omit to mention about the essence of travel is a small detail so obvious that one blushes to bring it up: namely, that every journey needs to start somewhere. A tourist leaves one country to visit another. A plane leaves one airport to land elsewhere. That the default setting on most online booking services assumes that you're going to want round-trip tickets suggests that every starting point is like the shadow partner of every arrival: the two have to be different—quite different—and their difference is what gives every journey its purpose. But for this difference, there is no curiosity, there is no travel, there are no tourists. Home is what sets the course to our travels. Home is what we leave behind, knowing we'll recover it at the end of the journey. Home is also what makes going away safe. To quote T. S. Eliot, "The end is where we start from." An odyssey is just a return trip that's taken too long.

By contrast, the travels of nomads or Gypsies belong to an altogether different category. Nomads roam the world, but their wandering is stirred not by curiosity but by practical survival. Nomads do not know where travel ends, inasmuch as none remembers where it started. There can be no voyage out, because there is no voyage back foreseen. There is no one place to travel back to. Traveling becomes the home, and errancy punctuates everything, from where nomads pray, wash their clothes, and seek food, to where they sleep at night and go to die. If a nomad pitches his tent in the exact same spot where he'd pitched it before, my guess is that it is either by coincidence or for the sake of convenience. The idea of returning to a particular place or of holding one place worthier than another for reasons that have nothing to do with material concerns seems a luxury if not a contradiction in terms. Nomads are indifferent to such things.

With exile, give both curiosity and indifference an extra torsion, then braid the two together, make sure both are thoroughly confused, and you'll understand how (or why) I travel.

I am an exile from Alexandria, Egypt.

Like the nomad, an exile is someone who has no home to go back to. He has lost his home; it's no longer there; there is no going back—Odysseus just got wind that Ithaca was entirely destroyed by an earthquake and that every person he knew there is gone. Unlike the nomad, though, an exile is not resigned to homelessness; perpetual transience feels as unnatural to him as it would to any tourist who's lost his return ticket. An exile wants a home, not a provisional rest stop. But having lost his home, he hasn't the foggiest notion how to go about finding a new one. He is even wary of having to "choose" a new home. Can one choose one's home any more than one can choose the color of one's skin? Anyone can build a house—but is it ever a home? Wherever he travels, he casts a wistful glance around, thinking to himself, "This is not how I remember things." "All this is very nice," he tells his traveling companion on glimpsing the Pacific Ocean, "but it's not the Mediterranean, and it feels so strange." He has no patience with the number-one rule of tourism: to seek the new, the unfamiliar, the different. "Of course it should feel strange and unfamiliar," says his traveling companion. "If you wanted familiar, you should have stayed home."

But this is precisely the problem. There is no home.

Home is altogether elsewhere.

Or, to use slightly different words, home is elsewhere in time—which is why exiles grow to like things that have *erstwhile* and *elsewhere* written all over them.

My wife, who was born and raised in the United States, travels with an exile when we go to Europe in the summer. She stares at this or that monument; I have no tolerance for monuments. She wants to stop by this or that small picturesque hill town; I care nothing for small picturesque hill towns. She visits churches and museums and is an inexhaustible font of curiosity. I am indifference personified. We walk the same streets but we might as well be walking on opposite sidewalks: she wants to see things she's never seen before; I can't wait to land on things I've known before.

She wants the new and the unfamiliar; I want nothing that isn't old. The last thing she wants is to be reminded of home; I can't wait to pick up remnants of mine. She likes to get lost; I still haven't found my way.

My curiosity, when I am indeed curious, is steered by a totally different agenda. Hers is based on seeing things that dazzle the imagination, mine on those that stir memory. We're traveling together separately.

I want to be reminded of the Ithaca I lost; she's after a new world. Every visit to a city on the Mediterranean needs to bring me closer to what I know, or to what I believe—but am no longer sure—I remember and think I want to revisit. Without this, I might as well not travel. I like to walk down the streets of foreign cities and spot imaginary signposts—unreal signposts that are real to me because they point to a parallel place and to a shadow time zone elsewhere in time.

My wife watches all this and tries to encourage me to unload the "baggage" I trail along. I know she is right. With her, sometimes, I walk down unfamiliar streets and try to meet her—as the saying goes—halfway. I look up at unimpressive residential buildings in nondescript neighborhoods and ask myself, not "Was this city worth visiting at all?" but "Could I live here?" I'm scoping out a home; she's happy with hotels.

Over the years we have reached a compromise of sorts: I will try not to travel in search of lost time; instead I will travel to seek out an imaginary future. I "connect," not by saying, "Isn't this little picturesque hill town beautiful?" but "Do I see myself living here?"

"Do I see myself as a child running down flights of stairs to head out to the movies with friends?"

"Do I see myself telling the corner baker to send up fresh bread tomorrow morning?"

"Do I hear the clatter of plates being set for long lunches with my entire family?"

Do I see myself living here? however, also asks an undisclosed and far too unsettling question: "Could I have lived here?"

I like to play with these two questions, for it is only by asking such questions that I "connect" with the world around me.

It is through this detour, this hope of restoring a remembered past in an imagined future that I come closest to what goes by the name of a comfort zone, call it a makeshift home, a counterfeit home. Grammarians might call this combination of past and future the imperfect conditional—otherwise known as a *contrafactual mood*. I am, come to think of it, a contrafactual tourist. I do not travel to see things; I come to prospect unreal time in unreal cities. It is only by finding a would-be, would-have-been, wannabe home that I begin to experience the joy that others feel when they go away. It is a transposed and counterintuitive joy, joy by proxy, the vicarious, artificial joy of finding in one place things lost in another.

And yet, should you dig a tiny bit deeper, it is no imaginary joy at all. It is a joy so real and so poignant that it summons feelings I never expected: the fear of being tempted by this new place I couldn't have cared less about or—more poignant yet—the fear of missing a place I flew to with no enthusiasm, no desire, and no curiosity and, at the last moment, ended up wanting to take back with me. It doesn't take long for me to see that what lies behind these fears goes by the name of one thing only—love—and that it is always love that catches us unawares, exiles, tourists, and nomads alike. We walk about a dreary town on a scalding hot day and as we're plotting the indifferent itinerary of a possible return trip in years to come, it suddenly hits us, as always obliquely, that this is love, isn't it? That it is really love we bring when we thought we were bringing nothing at all, that some of us find what is real for us through long and complicated detours when others find it staring right at them.

Roman Hours

Today, again, I stared at the small knife on my desk. I had purchased it months ago on the Campo de' Fiori, just before buying bread rolls and heading down the Via della Corda to find a quiet spot on the Piazza Farnese, where I sat on a stone ledge and made prosciutto and Bel Paese sandwiches. On the way to the Palazzo Farnese, I found a street fountain and rinsed a bunch of muscatel grapes I had bought from a *fruttivendolo*. I was leaning forward to cleanse the new knife as well, and to douse my face while I was at it, when it occurred to me that this, of all my days in Rome, was perhaps the one I would like most to remember, and that on this cheap knife—which I had originally planned to discard as soon as I was finished using it but had now decided to take back with me—was inscribed something of the warm, intimate feeling that settles around noon on typically clear Roman summer days. It came rushing to me in the form of a word—one word only, but the best possible word because it captured the weather, the city, and the mood on this most temperate day in June and, hence, of the year: *serenity*. Italians use the word *sereno* to describe the weather, the sky, the sea, a person. It means tranquil, clear, fair, calm.

And this is how I like to feel in Rome, and how the city feels when its languid ocher walls beam in the midday sun. When overbrimming old fountains dare you to dunk your hands in and splash your face and rest awhile before resuming your walk through yet narrower twisting lanes along the Campo Marzio in the *centro storico* (historic center) of Rome.

This warren of old alleys goes back many centuries, and here sinister brawls, vendettas, and killings were as common in the Renaissance as the artists, con artists, and other swaggerers who populated these streets. Today, these lanes with tilting buildings that have learned to lean on each other like Siamese twins exude a smell of slate, clay, and old dank limestone; the odor of wood glue and resin drift from artisans' shops, attesting to the timeless presence of workshops in the area. Otherwise, the streets are dead past midday. Except for bells, an occasional hammer, the sound of a lathe, or an electric saw that is no sooner heard than it's instantly silenced, the only sound you'll hear on the Vicolo del Polverone or the Piazza della Quercia is the occasional clatter of plates ringing from many homes, suggesting that lunch is about to be served in all Italy.

A few more steps into the Largo della Moretta, and suddenly you begin to make out the cool scent of roasted coffee emanating from hidden sanctuaries along the way. These havens—like tiny pilgrimage stations, or like the numerous churches to which men on the run, from Cellini to Tosca's Angelotti, rushed to seek asylum—each have their old legend. Caffè Rosati, Caffè Canova, Caffè Greco, Caffè Sant'Eustachio, Antico Caffè della Pace—small oases where blinding light and dark interiors go well together, the way hot coffee and lemon ice go well together, the way only Mediterraneans seek the shade and wait out the sun they love so much.

There is a magic to these summer hours that is as timeless as the tiny rituals we invent around them each day. Here are mine. Strolling in the dry heat and suddenly rediscovering the little-known Vicolo Montevecchio, where a huge, off-white *ombrellone* suddenly sprouts, spelling food and wine. Wasting yet another bottle of sparkling water by washing a hand unavoidably made sticky with food purchased on the fly. Baring both feet by the

Fontana delle Tartarughe in the Piazza Mattei, the empty square basking in the ocher glory of its adjoining buildings, and when no one's looking, letting them soak awhile in a pool of water so peaceful and translucent that not even the quietest beach on the quietest day could rival it.

Getting lost—the welcome sense that you are still unable to find your way in this maze of side streets—is something one never wishes to unlearn, because it means one's visit here is still very young. The rule is quite simple: scorn maps. They never show all Renaissance Rome anyway; they merely stand between you and the city. Stray instead. Enforced errancy and mild disconcertment are the best guide. Rome must swim before your eyes. You'll drift and wander and suddenly land, without knowing how, at the Piazza Navona, or the Campo de' Fiori, Sant'Andrea della Valle, the Pantheon, the Piazza di Spagna, or the Piazza del Popolo, with its stunning *tricorno* fanning out in three directions: the Via del Babuino, the Via del Corso, and the Via di Ripetta. "Could this be the Trevi Fountain?" you wonder, half fascinated by your internal compass, which knew all along where you were headed and which, in retrospect, gives you a sort of proprietary claim on the piazza, the way a prince may think he alone is entitled to marry a particular debutante simply because he was the first to spot her at court. How we discover beauty is not incidental to it; it prefigures it. The accident that brings us to the things we worship says as much about them as it does about us. What I want is not just to see the Turtle Fountain but to stumble upon the Turtle Fountain inadvertently.

This protean city is all about drifting and straying, and the shortest distance between two points is never a straight line but a figure eight. Just as Rome is not about one path, or about one past, but an accumulation of pasts: you encounter Gogol, Ovid, Piranesi, Ingres, Caesar, and Goethe on one walk; on another, Caravaggio and Casanova, Freud and Fellini, Montaigne and

Mussolini, James and Joyce; and on yet another, Wagner, Michel-angelo, Rossini, Keats, and Tasso. And you'll realize one more thing that nobody tells you: despite all these names, masonries, and landmarks, despite untold layers of stucco and plaster and paint slapped over the centuries on everything you see here, de-spite the fact that so many figures from one past keep surfacing in another, or that so many buildings are grafted onto generations of older buildings, what ultimately matters here are the inciden-tals, the small elusive pleasures of the senses—water, coffee, citrus, food, sunlight, voices, the touch of warm marble, glances stolen on the sly, and faces, the most beautiful in the world.

And this, without question, is the most beautiful city on earth, just as it is the most serene. Not only is the weather and everything around us serene, but we ourselves become serene. Serenity is the feeling of being one with the world, of having nothing to wish for, of lacking for nothing. Of being, as almost never happens elsewhere, entirely in the present. This, after all, is the most pagan city in the world; it is consumed by the present. The greatest sites and monuments, Rome tells us, mean nothing unless they stimulate and accommodate the body; unless, that is, we can eat, drink, and lounge among them. Beauty always gives pleasure, but in Rome, beauty is born of pleasure.

Twice a day, we come back to the Antico Caffè della Pace, off the Piazza Navona. The *caffè* is a few steps away from the Hotel Raphaël (a luxurious place whose roof garden offers an unim-peded view of the Campo Marzio). At the *caffè*, dashing would-be artists, models, drifters, and high-end wannabes sip coffee, read the paper, or congregate, which they do in greater numbers as the day wears on. I like to come here very early in the morning, when the scent of parched earth lingers upon the city, announcing warm weather and blinding glare toward noon. I like to be the first to sit down here, before the Romans have left their homes, because if I hate feeling that those who live here or were born after I'd left

Rome, years ago, have come to know my city better than I ever will, then being here before they're ready to face their own streets gives me some consolation. While I retain the privileged status of a tourist who doesn't have to go to work, I can easily pretend—an illusion sanctioned by jet lag—that I've never left Rome at all but just happened to wake up very early in the morning.

By evening, the jittery *caffè* crowd spills over into the street. Nearly everyone holds a *telefonino* in their hand, because they expect it to ring at any moment but also because it's part of the dress code, a descendant of the privileged dagger that conferred instant status at the unavoidable street brawl. One of these twenty- to thirty-year-olds sits at a table, staring attentively into his *telefonino* as though inspecting his features in a pocket mirror. Watching the flower of Rome, I see how easy it is to reconcile its cult of the *figura* with the beauty that abounds on a Baroque square such as the Piazza Navona. There will always remain something disturbingly enticing about this shady clientele. This, after all, is the universe of Cellini and Caravaggio. They lived, ate, brawled, loved, plotted, and dueled scarcely a few blocks away. Yet from some unknown cranny in their debauched and squalid lives, they gave the world the best it is ever likely to see. Here, as well, lived the ruthless Borgia pope Alexander VI, whose children Lucrezia Borgia and Cesare Borgia are notorious to history. A few steps away, and a hundred years later, Giordano Bruno was brought to the Campo de' Fiori, stripped naked, and burned at the stake. Scarcely a few months earlier, an event had taken place that shook Rome as probably nothing had since the martyring of the early Christians: the brutal decapitation of the beautiful young Beatrice Cenci by order of the pope himself.

We may never become Roman, and yet it takes no more than a few hours for the spell to kick in. We become different. Our gaze

starts to linger; we're less fussy over space; voices become more
interesting; smiles are over-the-counter affairs. We begin to see
beauty everywhere. We find it at Le Bateleur, a charming, run-
down antiques and curios shop on the Via di San Simone, off the
Via dei Coronari, where we find stunning French watercolors. Or at
Ai Monasteri, which sells products made in Italian monasteries
and where I found a delicious spiced grappa, the best Amaro,
and the sweetest honey I've ever known. Or at the Ferramenta alla
Chiesa Nuova, seemingly a hardware store but actually a knob,
door handle, and ancient keys gallery where people walk in bearing precious antique door hinges they despair of ever finding a
match for, only to have the owner produce a look-alike on the spot.

The city is beautiful in such unpredictable ways. The dirty
ocher walls (fast disappearing under new coats that restore their
original yellow, peach, pink, lilac) are beautiful. And why not?
Ocher is the closest stone will ever come to flesh; it is the color of
clay, and from clay God made flesh. The figs we're about to eat
under the sun are beautiful. The worn-out pavement along the
Via dei Cappellari is, however humble and streaked with dirt,
beautiful. The clarinetist who wends his way toward the sunless
Vicolo delle Grotte, wailing a Bellini aria, plays beautifully. The
Chiesa di Santa Barbara, overlooking Largo dei Librari, couldn't
offer a more accurate slice of a Roman *tableau vivant*, complete
with ice-cream vendor, sleeping dog, Harley-Davidson, canvas
ombrelloni, and men chatting in gallant fashion outside a small
haberdashery where someone is playing a mandolin rendition of
"Core 'ngrato," a Neapolitan song, while a lady wearing a series of
Felliniesque white voiles cuts across my field of vision. This sixty-
year-old aristocratic eccentric is, it takes me a second to realize,
speeding on a mountain bike, barefoot, with an air of unflappable
sprezzatura.

What wouldn't I give never to lose Rome. I worry, on leaving,
that like a cowered Cinderella returning to her stepmother's ser-

vice, I'll slip back into my day-to-day life far sooner than I
thought possible. It's not just the beauty that I'll miss. I'll miss,
too, the way this city gets under my skin and, for a while, makes
me its own, or the way I take pleasure for granted. It's a feeling I
wear with greater confidence every day. I know it is a borrowed
feeling—it's Rome's, not mine. I know it will go dead as soon as I
leave the Roman light behind.

This worry doesn't intrude on anything; it simply hovers, like a
needless safety warning to someone who's been granted immortal-
ity for a week. It was there when I purchased the ham, the rolls, the
knife. Or when I saw the Caravaggios in San Luigi dei Francesi;
or went to see Raphael's sibyls in Santa Maria della Pace but found
the door closed, and was just as pleased to admire its rounded col-
onnade instead. Could any of these timeless things really disappear from my life? And where do they go when I'm not there to
stare at them? What happens to life when we're not there to live it?

I first arrived in Rome as a refugee in 1965. Mourning my life in
Alexandria, and determined never to like Rome, I eventually sur-
rendered to the city, and for three magical years the Campo Marzio
was the place I came closest to ever loving. I grew to love Italian
and Dante, and here, as nowhere else on earth, I even chose the
exact building where I'd make my home someday.

Years ago, just where the Campo is split by the ostentatious
nineteenth-century thoroughfare, the Corso Vittorio Emanuele II,
I would start on one of two favorite walks. As soon as the school
bus had crossed the river from Vatican City, I'd ask the driver
to drop me at Largo Tassoni—rather than bring me all the way to
Stazione Termini, from where I'd have to take public transportation for another forty minutes before reaching our shabby apartment in a working-class neighborhood past Alberone. From
Largo Tassoni, either I would head south to the Via Giulia and

then the Campo de' Fiori, ambling for about two hours before finally going home, or I'd head north.

I liked nothing better than to lose my way in a labyrinth of tiny, shady, furtive, ocher-hued *vicoli*, which I hoped would one day, by dint of being strayed in, finally debouch into an enchanted little square where I'd encounter some still higher order of beauty. What I wished above all things was to amble freely about the streets of the Campo Marzio and to find whatever I wished to find there freely, whether it was the true image of this city, or something in me, or a likeness of myself in the things and people I saw, or a new home to replace the one I'd lost as a refugee.

Roaming about these streets past dark had more to do with me and my secret wishes than it did with the city. It allowed me to recast my fantasies each time, because this is also how we try to find ourselves—by hits and misses and mistaken turns. Dowsing around the Campo Marzio like a prospector was simply my way of belonging to this area and of claiming it by virtue of passing over it many, many times, the way dogs do when they mark their corners. In the aimlessness of my afternoon walks, I was charting a Rome of my own devising, a Rome I wanted to make sure did exist, because the one awaiting me at home was not the Rome I wanted. On the twilit lanes of a Renaissance Rome that stood between me and ancient Rome just as it stood between me and the modern world, I could pretend that any minute now, and without knowing how, I would rise out of one circle of time and, walking down a little lane lined by the mansions of the Campo Marzio, look through windows I had gotten to know quite well, ring a buzzer downstairs, and through the intercom hear someone's voice tell me that I was, once again, late for supper.

Then one afternoon, a miracle occurred. During a walk past the Piazza Campitelli, I spotted a sign on a door: AFFITTASI (to let).

Unable to resist, I walked into the building and spoke to the *portinaia*, saying that my family might be interested in renting the apartment. When told the price, I maintained a straight face. That evening, I immediately announced to my mother that we had to move and would she please drop everything the following afternoon and meet me after school to visit a new apartment. She did not have to worry about not speaking Italian; I would do all the talking. When she reminded me that we were poor now and relied on the kindness of relatives, I concocted an argument to persuade her that since the amount we paid a mean uncle each month for our current hole-in-the-wall was so absurdly bloated, why not find a better place altogether? To this day I do not know why my mother decided to play along. We agreed that if we couldn't persuade the *portinaia* to lower her price, my mother would make a face to suggest subdued disapproval.

I would never have believed that so run-down a façade on the Campo Marzio could house so sumptuous and majestic an apartment. As we entered the empty, high-ceilinged flat, our cautious, timid footsteps began to produce such loutish echoes on the squeaking parquet floor that I wished to squelch each one, as though they were escaped insects we had brought with us from Alberone that would give away our imposture. I looked around, looked at Mother. It must have dawned on both of us that we didn't even have enough money to buy a kitchen table for this place, let alone four chairs to go around it. And yet, as I peeked at the old rooms, this, I already knew, was the Rome I loved: thoroughly lavish and baroque, like a heroic opera by George Friedrich Handel. The *portinaia*'s daughter was following me with her eyes. I tried to look calm, and glanced at the ceiling as though inspecting it expertly, effortlessly. I slipped into another room. The bedrooms were too large. And there were four of them. I instantly picked mine. I looked out the window and spotted the familiar street. I opened the French windows and stepped out onto

a balcony, its tiles bathed in the fading light of the setting sun. I
leaned against the banister. *To live here.*

The people in the building across the street were watching
television. Someone was walking a dog on the cobbled side street.
Two large, glass streetlights hanging from both walls of an adjoining corner house had started to cast a pale orange glow upon
its walls. I imagined my mother sending me to buy milk downstairs, my dream scooter I'd park in the courtyard.

My mother had come well-dressed that day, probably to im-
press the *portinaia.* But her tailor-made suit, which had been
touched up recently, seemed dated, and she looked older, nervous. She played the part terribly, pretending there was something bothering her that she couldn't quite put her finger on, and
finally assuming the disappointed air we had rehearsed together
when it became clear that she and the *portinaia* could not agree
on the rent.

"*Anche a me dispiace, signore*—I too am sorry," said the *portinaia*'s daughter. What I took with me that day was not just the
regret in her dark, darting eyes as she escorted us downstairs,
but the profound sorrow with which, as if for good measure, she
had thrown in an unexpected bonus that stayed with me the rest
of my life: "*Signore.*" I had just turned fifteen.

I have often wondered what became of that apartment. After our
visit, I never dared pass it again and crafted elaborate detours to
avoid running into the *portinaia* or her daughter. Years later,
back from the States with long hair and a beard, I made my next
visit. What surprised me most was not that the Campo Marzio
was riddled with high-end boutiques, but that someone had taken
down the AFFITTASI sign and never put it up again. The apartment had not waited.

And yet the building I never lived in is the only place I revisit

each time I come back to Rome, just as the Rome that haunts
me still is the one I fabricated on my afternoon walks. Today, the
building is no longer drab ocher but peach pink. It too has gone
to the other side, and, like the girl with the blackamoor eyes, is
most likely trying to stay young, the expert touch of a beautician's
hand filling in those spots that have always humanized Roman
stone and made the passage of time here the painless, tiny miracle that it is. At fifteen, I visited the life I wished to lead and the
home I was going to make my own some day. Now, I was visiting
the life I had dreamed of living.

Fortunately, the present, like the noonday sun here, always
intrudes upon the past. Only seconds after I come to a stop before the building, a budding indifference takes hold of me and I
am hastening to start on one of those much-awaited long walks I
already know won't end before sundown. I am thinking of ocher
and water and fresh figs and the good, simple foods I'll have for
lunch. I am thinking of my large seventh-story balcony at the
Hotel de Russie, looking over the twin domes of Santa Maria di
Montesanto and Santa Maria dei Miracoli, off the Piazza del
Popolo. This is what I've always wished to do in Rome. Not visit
anything, not even remember anything, but just sit, and from my
perch, with the Pincio behind, scope the entire city lying before
me under the serene, spellbinding light of a Roman afternoon.

I am to go out tonight with old friends to a restaurant called
Vecchia Roma on the Piazza Campitelli. On our way, I know we'll
walk past my secret corner in the Campo Marzio—I always make
sure we take that route—where I'll throw a last, furtive look up at
this apartment by the evening light. An unreal spell always de-
scends upon Rome at night, and the large *lampadari* on these
empty, interconnecting streets beam with the light of small altars
and icons in dark churches. You can hear your own footsteps,
even though your feet don't seem to touch the ground but almost
hover above the gleaming slate pavements, covering distances

that make the span of years seem trivial. Along the way, as the streets grow progressively darker and emptier and spookier, I'll let everyone walk ahead of me, be alone awhile. I like to imagine the ghost of Leopardi, of Henri Beyle (known to the world as Stendhal), of Beatrice Cenci, of Anna Magnani, rising by the deserted corner, each one always willing to stop and greet me, like characters in Dante who have wandered up to the surface and are eager to mingle before ebbing back into the night. It is the Frenchman I'm closest to. He alone understands why these streets and the apartment up above are so important to me; he understands that coming back to places adds an annual ring and is the most accurate way of measuring time. He too kept coming back here. He smiles and adds that he's doing so still, reminding me that just because one's gone doesn't mean one loves this city any less, or that one stops fussing with time here once time stops everywhere else. This, after all, is the Eternal City. One never leaves. One can, if one wishes, choose one's ghost spot now. I know where mine is.

The Sea and Remembrance

I had hopes of heading off to the Lido by way of the Grand Canal this afternoon, but the water taxi I hired at the railway station has taken a strange turn. This will most likely spoil what I've been fantasizing about for months: taking in breathtaking views of all my favorite palazzi lining the city's waterway on the Grand Canal, before passing St. Mark's and then heading away from Venice at twice the speed toward the Lido. A long and narrow island some twenty minutes from the city, the Lido faces Venice and its lagoon on the western side; on the eastern side, where the Lido's shoreline dips into the Adriatic Sea, are its magnificent beaches.

As we're threading our intricate way through an unusually narrow canal not far from the train station, we keep slowing to negotiate rights of way—with another water taxi, with a gondola, and then with the large industrial barges stationed along the side of the canal that haul bags of cement, steel rods, and stone, even the rumbling debris of several buildings under renovation. I finally muster the courage to ask the driver how long he thinks our ride will take. But he is busy greeting friends on either side of a narrow bridge and doesn't hear me. Not that he could if he tried: there's too much going on—too many jackhammers, too much yelling. Venice is regentrifying before my eyes. "*Molto* trendy," someone had told me in Rome. "Venice is very trendy." The word *trendy* is trendy this year—Italians are using it constantly, sometimes in the superlative: *trendissimo.* "You'll have to be patient," my taxi driver answers me at last.

A few more turns and I find myself totally lost. To counter my driver's grimace and show it doesn't faze me in the least, I affect the weary nonchalance appropriate to jet-lagged travelers arriving too late to argue with underlings. Not a good beginning. I don't want to let my exchange in the water taxi spoil my arrival, but it has already dispelled the glistening Turner-Ruskin-Monet-Whistler moment I had choreographed for myself. I am reminded of Gustav von Aschenbach, the stiff, fastidious, well-groomed, unbohemian writer in Thomas Mann's novella *Death in Venice,* who arrives in the city and is taken to the Lido not by vaporetto, as he had requested, but by gondola: a minor altercation ensues between the incensed German tourist and the headstrong gondolier, until the passenger is finally persuaded that there is really nothing to do but sit quietly and wait till he reaches his destination. In Luchino Visconti's 1971 film adaptation of Mann's novella, Aschenbach's arrival in Venice is accompanied by Gustav Mahler's Fifth Symphony, which is ideally suited to the occasion. Tension and premonition are brewing beneath, but on the surface is only the most serene, unruffled strains of Mahler's Adagietto strumming to Mann's "splashing of the oar as the wave struck dull against the prow."

Within moments, however, we're on none other than the Grand Canal itself—which means that the lagoon is still quite a stretch away and we haven't even reached St. Mark's yet. Suddenly I experience both the joy of averting a confrontation with the driver and the absolute bliss of catching sight of an expanse of seawater I've given up hope of ever seeing again. From here, even I could steer our way to the Lido. I am almost tempted to ask the driver to let me handle the wheel for a few seconds. But I'd better not. Better sit back and let this water city, like all water cities, take its time and come to me.

Water cities have a way of seducing us, though it's always difficult to know why, and explanations vary with each city. Perhaps
it's the fact that when afternoons grow too hot and the air too
thick, you can always turn your back on your day-to-day life, ut-
ter an exasperated "Enough with this," pull out a bathing suit
stashed somewhere in your desk, and dash off to the nearest
beach. Unlike in cities where beaches lie an hour from home, in
Venice water is available before you ever long for it: the lines between work and play, downtown and resort town, blur. Here, water is a part of life, of who you are, of everything you take for
granted, of what you do, eat, and smell. Water cities are like conditional, transient homes; they are our romance with the sea,
with time, with space, with ourselves.

Marseille, Barcelona, Trieste, Istanbul—each romances the
Mediterranean in its own fashion, mostly by embracing the sea in
sweeping C-shaped bays that date back to antiquity. But none has
gone beyond romance and literally consented to everlasting mat-
rimony, as Venice has. Here, the nuptials of city and sea are cel-
ebrated each year on the Sunday after the Feast of the Ascension,
when the doge of Venice throws a symbolic ring into the sea a
short distance from the Lido. Where the sea is, so is the city.

There is no spot in Venice where one can't see the sea, or is
not aware of it, or does not worry about it or respond to it. At
dawn, at night, in winter and summer, and during the quieter
hours of the afternoon, you can always hear the lazy slap of water
lapping the stone walls of the canals, licking and ticking like the
pulse of the city. As for the smell, it never goes away. Even in the
morning, when fresh air is hauled in like produce from the main-
land, the smell is there: between sea salt, marine growth, and
diesel fuel, something brackish always hovers over Venice.

The smell is more pungent here than anything in Genoa,
Naples, or Rimini, perhaps because Venice is all standing water:
slushy, bilgy, dirty—an open sewer, some have remarked. The

back alleys of Venice, narrow and grubby, spill easily into the canals, and many a time you can catch an elegant Venetian picking up his dog's droppings in a newspaper, rolling up the contents, and then, instead of throwing them away in the many overstuffed rubbish bins along the city's *campi*, tossing the little package with grandiloquent *menefreghismo* right into the Grand Canal.

The lavish palazzi lining the canal are no better. Although they may spell more opulence per square inch than anywhere in the world, and their ancient glass panels may shimmer—reminders that the one thing wealth likes best is to be stared at and envied— each is dangerously close to going under. Everything is so frail here. Palaces stand together like majestic old dowagers with rotting teeth and magnificent hairdos who do not fall partly because they've learned to lean together for support but also because, despite their squat, wizened forefronts, they possess the weary certainty of the aging rich who know that they're not going anywhere. You, however, are just passing through.

But this is no Potemkin village. The façades of the palazzi don't come close to what's inside. And yet beyond their stately interiors are dark, barren courtyards to remind you that Venetian wealth has humble and makeshift origins. Their bricks are ingots of history, cluttered, crammed, packed together; if each one could speak, Venice, despite its reputation for inventing the art of sotto voce, would be the loudest city on earth. Unlike Neapolitans, Venetians are by temperament quiet (they have to be; they live on top of one another) and secretive. It is why the city exudes something at once cagey and sinister—its "hateful sultriness" and "stagnating air," in Mann's words. Here, after all, excelled that literary genre called the unsigned denunciation. This is a place made for Pulcinella, pantomime, and Henry James. Bruised and brooding characters, speaking in half-whispers, thrive along gloomy *calli*, the intricate side alleys.

Within the space of a few years, James, Proust, and Mann felt

the dark pull of the city, which stirred their lofty aesthetic sentiments as well as their appreciation for abject sleaze. Venice, wrote
Mann, is "half fairy tale, half snare," a bifurcation echoed in Jan
Morris's description: "half eastern, half western, half land, half
sea, poised between Rome and Byzantium, between Christianity
and Islam, one foot in Europe, the other paddling in the pearls of
Asia."

Facing the Adriatic Sea, the Lido could be considered the
result of the pragmatic Venetian imagination gone wild; it began
as a successful pre–World War I financial venture that produced
two of Europe's finest hotels, a leisurely lifestyle quite unlike the
fretful pace found in Venice, and a small beach-resort town where
people come to swim by day and party by night. It is difficult to
imagine a Lido without Venice playing host to it, but once you've
seen the Lido (which not all tourists know they should), it becomes equally difficult to imagine a Venice without the beaches.

I first saw the Hôtel des Bains and the Excelsior years ago. I
had taken the vaporetto directly from the train station, disembark-
ing at the Piazzale Santa Maria Elisabetta on the Lido, on what
must have been the very same spot where, in Visconti's film, the
tricky gondolier lets off Aschenbach before absconding back to
Venice. From the dock, I had followed Aschenbach's path down
the Gran Viale Santa Maria Elisabetta, "that white-blossoming
avenue with taverns, booths, and pensions on either side [of] it,
which runs across the island diagonally to the beach," as Mann
described it, until I reached the shore, not far from the Hôtel des
Bains, which is situated on the Lungomare Marconi.

The Hôtel des Bains looks out to the Adriatic Sea, as does the
Excelsior, another equally majestic hotel on the same *lungomare*,
or promenade. Both reflect the wealth and grandeur of a world
whose inhabitants would just as readily have booked first-class
tickets on the *Orient-Express* or sailed out of Southampton on the
Titanic. The Hôtel des Bains is built in a sober and understated

Art Nouveau style, while the Excelsior, which opened its doors in 1907, is more flamboyant, with a long Moorish-Venetian façade. No more than a ten-minute walk apart, the two are connected by a shuttle bus that makes a perpetual loop between them. A tiny canal from the lagoon leads to the Excelsior's private dock, from which a water taxi departs every thirty minutes, shuttling between the Excelsior and the Hotel Danieli, near St. Mark's Square.

Along with the Danieli, Venice boasts three other superb hotels: the Cipriani, the Gritti, and the Bauer. Normally, a city will give birth to tourist establishments. On the Lido it's the other way around. The Hôtel des Bains and the Excelsior essentially created the Lido. Lord Byron rode horses on the empty stretches of beach, and there is an old Jewish cemetery here. But whatever the character of the island before the hotels, it was permanently changed by the tourist industry. Here, before World War I—Europe's rudest awakening ever—the pre-1914 royalty and high society came to summer and partake of swimming, a fad that had seized the Western imagination in the latter decades of the previous century. Here, flush from a great day on the beach, where they had bathed and dried themselves and lounged on striped chaise longues under rows of canopies, members of the high bourgeoisie spiffed themselves up and waited for dinner to be served, doing their utmost to convince others and themselves that their blood had acquired a tinge of blue.

Those days are long gone. We may come to Venice and the Lido chasing sepia memories from bygone days, but we will never find the same setting, the same habits, the same patter of waiters' deferential footsteps. Yet we are reluctant to replace our daguerreotype vision of Visconti's stylishly choreographed breakfast scene at the Hôtel des Bains with the dressed-down, barefoot, come-as-you-are, all-you-can-eat mêlée of parents and children that it is today. In the back of our minds, we still hope that the miracle will occur: sitting alone on the veranda facing the sea one evening, we'll somehow find ourselves drifting into the stately grandeur of a fin de siècle world—a world unaware that it is hurtling toward the conflict that will end it. Thomas Mann's novella was published in 1912. The guns of August came two summers later.

The Great War may have stunned the world, but within a few years, the magnates, tycoons, and movie stars came back to the Lido. They disappeared again during World War II—only to return once more. They have not vanished a third time. Since the post-war reinstallation of the Venice Film Festival in 1949, the Lido has retained an aura of jet-set exclusivity that appeals to the very wealthy, the wannabes, and the not-so-wealthy beneficiaries of sub-rosa promotional rates. People come here to mingle with movie stars. Or they come here knowing that they will stay in a room that was occupied by one. Or they come to feel like one. Or they come for Thomas Mann. But everyone comes for the sea.

For this, of all the spots in Venice, is where everyone can literally dip their toes into water. The Grand Canal, like the rivers ringing Manhattan, is off-limits: murky, gray-green, lusterless. The water on the Lido, however, is always calm, alternating between slate green and light blue. You can wade into it and walk a great distance before it touches your knees; even then, the Adriatic is clement and, with hardly any undertow, easy to swim. Far out in these waters, you can allow your mind to wander until all you see is the diminutive outline of the hotel at whose beach you're swimming. The Hôtel des Bains and the Excelsior have a partnership, and by showing a pass at either, you can swim in the pool or at the beach, or rent a beach cabana and sit in the shade. The scene hasn't changed since Mann described it in 1911:

> The shallow gray sea was already gay with children wading, with swimmers, with figures in bright colors lying on the sandbanks with arms behind their heads. Some were rowing in little keelless boats painted red and blue, and

laughing when they capsized. A long row of *capanni* ran
down the beach, with platforms, where people sat as on
verandas, and there was social life, with bustle and with
indolent repose; visits were paid, amid much chatter,
punctilious morning toilettes hobnobbed with comfortable and privileged dishabille. On the hard wet sand close
to the sea figures in white bathrobes or loose wrappings
in garish colors strolled up and down.

But it is the water that I love most. The anticipation begins as
soon as I land at the Excelsior's dock, then builds as I check in
and am shown to my room. The bellhop, waiting for his tip, sets
down my luggage, showcases the minibar, and explains the work-
ings of the thermostat and the television set. Then, knowing this
is the most luminous moment of all—like a street performer who
hits the high C while his assistant makes the rounds with an
empty bowler hat—he throws open the window overlooking the
beach. There is a sudden influx of muffled sounds—the surf below,
children at play, arguments—and a bold, rough, telltale smell of
salt that does not go well with the dormant, well-kept room, which
is at once sheltered and sheltering and which bears the soothing
floral scent of well-starched cotton sheets, choice detergents, and
cleaning fluids. Sea fever. Five minutes later, with or without jet
lag, I will find my way to the beach. I know where I've packed my
bathing suit and my beach thongs. It's late in the afternoon. Swims
at this hour belong to those who live on the beach, not to those
who must return to the city or who are desperately stuffing their
days with tourist activities. These swims—when the water is warm
and the beach is almost empty and the beach-keepers have started
sweeping the sand—can stretch past sunset. It is in those moments
that I realize the ultimate illusion, the ultimate luxury: I can
imagine that this is my city, my beach, my home.
   The Lido is the best way to experience Venice. Venice is a

crowded city, and on hot summer days the weather is unbearable: the sirocco, the desert wind, steals the breath from your lungs. On hot days, there is nowhere to sit in Venice unless it's in a restaurant or a café or on the edge of a scalding cistern. Nor is there respite from the crowds that, like toothpaste squeezed out of a tube, push through the narrow passageways that join one *campo* to another. What good is having the sea all around you if you can't even touch it on such days? On the Lido, though, I can spend half a day at my hotel, on the beach or in the large swimming pool, and then get on the shuttle boat and in twenty minutes be standing in St. Mark's Square. After dinner, I can hop the shuttle and be back at the Excelsior in no time.

And if I should miss the last shuttle, then, failing a water taxi, I'll take the final vaporetto from Venice, sit back, and, as I did years ago, watch the moonlit water-city sparkle in the dark. I'll lean on the railing of the speeding ferry boat and stare at the lagoon and watch the Lido draw nearer, until it will be time to get off at the Piazzale Santa Maria Elisabetta, as I did the first time I came here looking for the bygone luxury of a bygone world. I'll walk down the Gran Viale toward the beach, turn right along my beloved *lungomare*, and, if I'm in the mood, keep walking past the Hôtel des Bains: the view of the quiet Adriatic Sea in the dark of night is nothing short of breathtaking.

But before reaching the promenade, I might decide to stay on the Viale. It is flanked by several hotels and large, vibrant alfresco trattorias, as well as many ice-cream stands where the local folk sit around tables, three generations crammed together, their chairs spilling into the street. I like to walk up and down the Gran Viale in the evening because it reminds me that, try as I wish to see the ghosts of a late-nineteenth-century world, that world is destined to evade me. It may no longer exist except in books and films and in our collective imagination—layer upon layer of images, starting in 1907, when the Excelsior was built;

then skipping to 1912, when Mann's novella was published; then
to Visconti's 1971 film; and on to Benjamin Britten's 1973 opera
of the same name. I add to these, of course, memories of my own
trips here; they haunt my swims and my strolls along the *lungomare*. As I try to understand why it is so difficult for me to define
this sense of near-total bliss that is never total enough, I recall
Henry James's prescient words. The important thing about Venice, he wrote in *Italian Hours*, is "to linger and remain and
return."

And so I like the simplicity of the Gran Viale, with its permanently closed Fascist-style casino, next to which the Venice Film
Festival marks the end of each summer. I like how the Gran Viale
contrasts with the magnificence of the two hotels. Perhaps I need
this contrast. I need it to remember that what I hope to find here
each time no longer exists, that this is just a hotel, that this is just
a beach resort. And having made my peace with my century, I
can come in from the garden, climb the wide staircase, and catch
myself thinking, if only for a split second: This is not me now,
this is someone else—someone who will sit on the balcony, order
a drink, and for a while at least, as he looks to the horizon, think
that there is not a thing more to want in life.

Place des Vosges

Even today, after many years, there are moments when your eyes could almost be fooled—when they'll still believe that however you wandered into this huge quadrangle called the Place des Vosges, you'll never find your way out. Wherever you turn your gaze, this mini-Paris in the heart of old Paris, and perhaps the most beautiful urban spot in the world, seems to turn its back not just on the rest of the world but on the rest of Paris as well. You step in—and time stops.

At night, when the Place des Vosges grows quiet and traffic comes to a halt, the arched entrances under the Pavillons du Roi and de la Reine blend into the darkness, as do the two narrow side streets tucked to the northeast and northwest of the Place, the rue des Francs-Bourgeois and the rue du Pas-de-la-Mule. With no apparent means out, it is impossible not to feel that you are indeed back in this self-contained, self-sufficient seventeenth-century enclave, just as the original founders of the square, four hundred years ago, wished to be locked in a Paris of their own devising—a Paris that had the very best of Paris, a Paris that hadn't quite been invented yet and of which this was a promise. Recent restoration has been so successful that the Place looks better today than it has in three centuries and gives a very good picture of the Paris its ancien régime founders envisioned.

On the Place des Vosges, you can almost touch old Paris. At midnight, upon leaving L'Ambroisie (at no. 9)—among the best

and most expensive restaurants in Paris, in the building where
Louis XIII stayed during the 1612 inauguration of the square—
you don't just step into seventeenth-century Paris but into a Paris
where the eighteenth and nineteenth centuries are superimposed
over earlier and later times no less beguilingly than Atget's *vieux*
Paris photos can still cast albuminous sepia tones over today's
Paris. The footsteps heard along the dark arcades may not even
belong to a living soul but to shadows from the past—say, Victor
Hugo, who lived at 6 Place des Vosges between 1832 and 1848,
or Cardinal Richelieu, who two centuries earlier lived diagonally
across the square (at no. 21), or the occasional ruffian who would
turn up in this affluent enclave and terrorize the ladies. Turn
around and you might just as easily spot the fleeting silhouette of
the notorious seventeenth-century courtesan Marion Delorme
(at no. 11), heading home under the cover of the arcades; or of
France's most illustrious preacher, Bossuet (at no. 17); or of Madame de Rambouillet (at no. 15), whose salon was a who's who of
seventeenth-century France. Delorme had been Cardinal Richelieu's mistress once but was now accompanied by Cardinal de
Retz, one of France's most devoted ladies' men. A habitué of the
Place des Vosges, Retz, the turbulent antimonarchist, had been the
lover of both Marie-Charlotte de Balzac d'Entragues (at no. 23)
and the Princesse de Guéméné (at no. 6).

Many aristocratic ladies who lived on the square and around
the Marais were known as *précieuses*: women who adopted an
overrefined, highly conceited form of speech that, despite their
cultivated delicacy in attitude and taste, by no means entailed an
equally cultivated sense of morality. They frequently had several
lovers, and the Princesse de Guéméné was no exception. She
loved the unruly Count of Montmorency-Boutteville, who had
also been the lover of Madame de Sablé (at no. 5) and who, following a terrible *duel à six* in 1627 in front of the home of Cardinal Richelieu (who had made dueling a capital offense in France),

was subsequently captured and beheaded. Such would be the fate of two of the Princesse's other lovers.

Nothing better illustrates these crisscrossed, overlapping, and at times simultaneous passions than the loves of another *précieuse*, Marguerite de Béthune (at no. 18). She was the daughter of the Duc de Sully, King Henry IV's superintendent of finances, who was instrumental in planning the Place des Vosges (his Hôtel de Sully still feeds into the Place through a tiny, near-inconspicuous door at no. 7). Marguerite had been the mistress of both the Duc de Candale (at no. 12) and the Marquis d'Aumont (at no. 13). Since the even numbers on the Place des Vosges are located to the east of the Pavillon du Roi, and the odd to the west, it is possible to suppose that when she was with one she could easily manage to think of, if not spy on, the other.

Throughout its history, the very thought of the Place des Vosges has instantly conjured images of grand passion and grand intrigue. The importance that the Place des Vosges has in the French imagination, like that of Versailles, may explain why French literature, from the seventeenth century on, has never quite been able to disentangle love from its surrogate, double-dealing, or courtship from diplomacy, underscored as they all are by the cruelest and crudest form of self-interest. Such irony escaped no one, and certainly not the disabused courtiers of *précieux* society.

Few of them had anything kind to say about love or about the women they loved. Cardinal de Retz's racy and tempestuous *Mémoires* were most exquisitely vicious in this regard. (Of his ex-mistress Madame de Montbazon, he wrote, "I have never known anyone who, in her vices, managed to have so little regard for virtue.") And yet his *Mémoires* are dedicated to one of the *précieux* world's busiest writers, his good friend Madame de Sévigné, born at 1 bis Place des Vosges. Sévigné was herself a very close friend of the Duchesse de Longueville, Madame de Sablé, the Duc de La Rochefoucauld, and Madame de La Fayette, the author of Europe's first modern novel, *La Princesse de Clèves*. To show how intricately interwoven this world was, one has only to recall that La Rochefoucauld may have had a platonic relationship with La Fayette but he most certainly did not with the Duchesse de Longueville, with whom he had a son and for whom the disillusioned and embittered La Rochefoucauld probably continued to ache until the very end of his days. Known as one of the most beautiful women of the period, the fair-haired Duchesse led as blustery a life as Cardinal de Retz—first as a lover, then as a warrior, and finally as a religious woman. It was because of her bitter feud with her rival, Madame de Montbazon, that another duel took place on the square, between descendants of the Guise and the Coligny families. Each man may have gallantly taken the side of one of the two women, but after about a century of feuding between the Catholic Guises and the Protestant Colignys there was enough gall for another duel. It took Coligny almost five months to die of his wounds. It is said that the Duchesse de Longueville watched the duel from the windows of 18 Place des Vosges, the home of Marguerite de Béthune, the woman whose lovers' pavilions faced each other. The quarrel between the Duchesse de Longueville and Madame de Montbazon reads like a novel filled with slander, malice, jealousy, and spite.

Scandalmongering was a favorite occupation, and the preferred weapon was not so much the sword as the letter: dropped, intercepted, recopied, falsely attributed, and purloined letters were ferried back and forth, leaving a trail that invariably led to the loss of reputations and, just as frequently, of life—Coligny's in this instance—and ultimately to civil unrest. At the risk of oversimplifying, tensions mounted to such a pitch that many of those who had anything to do with the Place des Vosges before the middle of the seventeenth century eventually joined the Fronde, the antimonarchist aristocratic campaign of 1648–53. It was the last aristocratic revolt against the monarchy, and Louis XIV, the Sun

King, never forgot it. To ensure that the aristocracy never again rose against him, he made certain that almost every one of its members moved to Versailles.

Like its storied residents, the Place des Vosges remains a tangle of the most capricious twists in urban memory. Known initially as the Place Royale in 1605, it became the Place des Fédérés after the Revolution in 1792; the Place de l'Indivisibilité in 1793; and then the Place des Vosges in 1800, under Napoléon. It resumed its first name in 1814, after the restoration of the monarchy, and lost it once more to the Place des Vosges in 1831. After yet another revolution, it became once again the Place Royale in 1852, and finally the Place des Vosges in 1870. The Place teemed with intellectuals, writers, aristocrats, salons, and courtesans. It witnessed generations of schemes, rivalries, and duels, the most famous of these being the duel of 1614, known as "the night of the torches," between the Marquis de Rouillac and Philippe Hurault, each flanked by his second, everyone wielding a sword in one hand and a blazing torch in the other. Three were killed; Rouillac alone survived, and lived thereafter at 2 Place des Vosges.

I come to the Place des Vosges to make believe that I belong, that this could easily become my home. Paris is too large a city, and time is too scarce for me to ever become a full resident—but this square is just right. After a few days, I am at home. I know every corner, every restaurant, and every grocer and bookstore beyond the square. Even faces grow familiar, as does the repertoire of the high-end street entertainers and singers who come to perform under the arcades every Saturday: the pair singing duets by Mozart, the tango and fox-trot dancers, the Baroque ensembles, the pseudo-Django jazz guitarist, and the eeriest countertenor—mock castrato bel canto singer I've ever heard, each standing behind stacks of their own CDs.

For lunch, I've grown to like La Mule du Pape on the rue du Pas-de-la-Mule, scarcely off the square: light fare, fresh salads, excellent desserts. And early in the morning, I like to come to Ma Bourgogne, on the northwest corner of the square, and have breakfast outside, under the arcades. I've been here three times already, and I am always among the first to sit down. I think I have my table now, and the waiter knows I like *café crème* and a buttered baguette with today's jam. I even get here before the bread arrives from the baker's. I sit at the corner of this empty square and watch schoolboys plod their way diagonally across the park, one after the other, sometimes in pairs or clusters, each carrying a heavy satchel or a briefcase strapped around his shoulders. I can easily see my sons doing this. Yes, it does feel right. Then, just as I am getting used to the square and am busily making it my home—tarts, salads, fresh produce, baguette, jam, coffee—I look up, spot the imposing row of redbrick pavilions with their large French windows and slate roofs, and realize that this, as I always knew but had managed to forget, is the most beautiful spot in the civilized world.

Parisians, of course, have always known this, and during the seventeenth and eighteenth centuries routinely overwhelmed foreign dignitaries by escorting them to the Place before returning them to the business of their visit. What must have struck these foreigners was something perhaps more dazzling and arresting than French magnificence or French architecture. For the Place des Vosges is not magnificent in the way that, say, Versailles or the Louvre or the Palais-Royal is magnificent. And the thirty-six cloned, slate-roofed, redbrick, and limestone "row house" pavilions—with the interconnecting arcades, or *promenoirs,* running the length of all four sidewalks of a square no larger than the size of a Manhattan city block—can by no stretch of the imagination be called a miracle of seventeenth-century architecture. As with any *cour carrée,* what is striking is not necessarily each unit but the repetition thirty-six times of the same unit, many of which already boast a small square courtyard within. It is the symmetry of the square that casts a spell, not each segment—except that here the symmetry is projected on so grand a scale that it ends up being as disorienting and as humbling as quadratic symmetry is in Descartes or contrapuntal harmonies in Bach. If the French have nursed an unflagging fondness for Cartesian models, it is not because they thought nature was framed in quadrants but, rather, because their desire to fathom it, to harness it, and ultimately to explain it as best they could led them to chop up everything into pairs and units of two. Drawing and quartering may have been one of the worst forms of execution, but the French mania for symmetry has also given us palaces and gardens and the most spectacular urban planning imaginable, the way it gave us something that the French have treasured since long before the Enlightenment and of which they are still unable to divest themselves even when they pretend to try: a passion for clarity.

It is hard to think of anyone who lived on or around the Place des Vosges during the first half of the seventeenth century who didn't treasure this one passion above all others. Even in their loves—hapless and tumultuous and so profoundly tragic as they almost always turned out to be—the French displayed intense level-headedness when they came to write about them. They had to dissect what they felt, or what they remembered feeling, or what they feared others thought about their feelings. They were intellectuals in the purest—and perhaps coarsest—sense of the word. It was not what they saw that was clear; human passions seldom are. It was how they expressed what they saw that was so fiercely lucid. In the end, they preferred dissecting human foibles to doing anything about them. They chatted their way from one salon to the next, and on the Place des Vosges this was not difficult to do. Almost every pavilion on the square had a *précieuse* eager to host her little salon, or *ruelle*, in her bedroom. It is difficult to know whether there was more action than talk in these intimate *ruelles*. What is known is that everyone excelled at turning everything into talk. They intellectualized everything.

As Descartes had done in *The Passions of the Soul*, they charted the progress of love on a geometrical plane that is so frightfully balanced that one suspects they needed these models the better to dispel the chaos within them. Love maps such as Mademoiselle de Scudéry's *carte de Tendre* are still found in many poster shops in Paris. Ironic and obscene versions of Scudéry's somewhat righteous map were not slow to crop up. One of them makes Place Royale the very capital of coquettish love. Yet another was penned by Bussy-Rabutin, Madame de Sévigné's cousin. Nothing could better spell the difference between the French and the British than the fact that while the French were busily charting out their version of Vanity Fair, across the channel a puritan by the name of John Bunyan was busily mapping out a journey of an entirely different order. Bunyan's *Pilgrim's Progress* appeared in the same year as did Madame de La Fayette's *Princesse de Clèves*. One saw the world as good and evil; the other saw it as a series of psychological twists and turns that brings to mind the analytical mania that became fashionable in the many, many salons on the Place des Vosges.

The French had a name for this. They called it *préciosité*. It was their way of giving their best quality a bad name. Eventually, they thought better of themselves and called it Classicism. Either way, they had caught the bug, and never again would the French resist digging out doubts and calling each one by its full name: *je ne sais quoi*—literally: I-don't-know-what. Nothing delighted them more than smoking out truth with a *je ne sais quoi*. The mixing of Descartes and Mannerism yielded sumptuous results.

Charles Le Brun, an ardent disciple of Descartes, remains one of the principal decorators of the Place des Vosges. His style is frequently considered Baroque; yet few would argue that if anything was alien to the Baroque sensibility it was Cartesian thinking. On the Place des Vosges, the dominance of intellect over excess is never hard to detect. Yet there are still telltale signs of sublimated trouble. The street level and first and second floors of

every pavilion may have been the picture of architectural harmony and built according to very strict specification—there were
to be no deviations from the model supplied by King Henry IV's
designers (often thought to be Androuet du Cerceau and Claude
Chastillion)—but the dormer windows on the top floors do not always match: they are each builder's tiny insurrection against the
master plan.

Henry IV, who favored the building of the Place, remains the
most beloved French king: *le bon roi* or *le vert galant* (the ladies'
man), as he is traditionally called, famous for his wit, good cheer,
sound judgment, and all-around hearty appetite. Every French
peasant, he said, would have a chicken in his pot each Sunday.
When told that he could become a French king provided he con-
verted from Protestantism to Catholicism he did not bat an eye-
lash. Paris, he declared, was well worth a Mass. Like the Place
Dauphine, the square's cousin on the Île de la Cité, the Place des
Vosges is built in a style that is recognizably Henry IV: all brick-
and-stone facings, brick being, like the personality of Henry IV,
down-to-earth, practical, basic, made for all times and all sea-
sons. Though the Place des Vosges is elegant and posh, and is
hardly spare, there is nothing palatial here. It also reflects the
spirit of the high-ranking officials, entrepreneurs, and financiers
to whom the king and his finance minister, Sully, had parceled
out the land in 1605 on condition that each build a home at his
own expense, according to a predetermined design. Some of them
were born rich; others had made vast fortunes and, no doubt,
intended both to keep them and to flaunt them. But like their
king, they were neither garish nor gaudy: wealth hadn't gone to
their heads, just as power hadn't gone to their king's. Both forms
of intoxication were due to happen, of course, but in another generation and under a very different monarch: Henry's grandson
Louis XIV.

The grounds on which Henry IV decided to build the new
square had once been the site of the Hôtel des Tournelles, famous

for its turrets, and where King Henry II had died in 1559 as a result of a wound inflicted during a friendly joust with a man bearing the rather foreign-sounding name of Gabriel de Montgomery. Following Henry II's death, his wife, Catherine de Médicis, had the Hôtel des Tournelles razed. To this day, Catherine is regarded as a mean, cunning, and vindictive queen, whose ugliest deed was the St. Bartholomew's Day Massacre of 1572, during which hundreds of French Protestants were put to the sword. It is another one of those ironies of history that the Protestant Henry IV, who had hoped to placate French Catholics by marrying Catherine and Henry II's daughter Queen Margot, was not only unable to forestall the massacre, which erupted immediately after his wedding, but would himself be felled by a religious fanatic forty years later a few blocks from where Henry II had died. He thus did not live to see his square completed.

Henry IV and Sully were far too practical to be called visionaries, but surely there must have been something of the visionary in each. They had originally intended the arcades to house common tradesmen, cloth manufacturers, and skilled foreign workers, most likely subsidized by the government. The idea was a good one, since Sully, like France's other finance ministers, had had the wisdom to attract foreign workers to help France produce domestically and ultimately export what it would otherwise have had to purchase abroad. But in this case it proved too impractical. This, after all, was prime real estate. It was so exclusive an area that, rather than design a square whose buildings would boast façades looking out on the rest of Paris, the planners turned these elegant storefronts in on themselves—as though the enjoyment of façades were reserved not for the passerby, who might never even suspect the existence of this secluded Place, but strictly for the happy few.

The Place des Vosges has all the makings of a luxurious courtyard turned outside in, which is exactly what Corneille saw in his comedy *La Place royale*. Everyone lives close together, everyone moves in the same circles, and everyone knows everyone else's business. Look out your window and you'll spy everyone's dirty laundry. And yet don't be so sure, either: as Madame de Lafayette said of life at court, here nothing is ever as it seems. The Place des Vosges was, as Corneille had instantly guessed, not just the ideal gold coast but also the ideal stage.

None of the residents, however, had any doubt that they belonged at the center of the universe. They were prickly, caustic, arrogant, querulous, spiteful, frivolous, urbane, and, above all things, as self-centered as they ultimately turned out to be self-hating. Like the square itself, this world was so turned in on itself that if it was consumed by artifice, it was just as driven by the most corrosive and disquieting forms of introspection. No society, not even the ancient Greeks, had ever sliced itself open so neatly, so squarely, to peek into the mouth of the volcano, and then stood there frozen, gaping at its worst chimeras. They may have frolicked in public, but most were pessimists through and through. The irony that they shot at the world was nothing compared with that which they saved for themselves.

La Rochefoucauld, who wrote in the most chiseled sentences known to history, expressed this better than any of his contemporaries. His maxims are short, penetrating, and damning. "Our virtues are most frequently nothing but vices disguised." "We always like those who admire us: we do not always like those whom we admire." "If we had no faults, we would not take so much pleasure in noticing them in others." "We confess our little faults only to conceal our larger ones." "In the misfortune of our best friends, we find something that is not unpleasing."

It is hard to hear the echo of so much pessimism or intrigue on the square today. Art galleries, shops, restaurants, and even a tiny synagogue and a nursery school line the arcades. Access to the

Place des Vosges is no longer restricted to those who possess a key—which used to be the case. Now, on a warm summer afternoon, one of the four manicured lawns—French gardens are always divided into four parts—is made available to the public, and here, lovers and parents with strollers can lounge about on the green in a manner that is still not quite characteristically Parisian. The Place lies at the heart of cultural activity in the Marais. Two blocks away is the Bastille Opera House; a few blocks west is the Musée Carnavalet; to the north, the Jewish Museum and the Picasso Museum. The rue Vieille-du-Temple, one of the most picturesque streets in the Marais, crosses what is still a Jewish neighborhood.

In the evening, the square teems with people who remind me that the SoHo look is either originally French or the latest export from New York. In either case, it suggests that everything is instantly globalized in today's world. And yet, scratch the surface . . . and it's still all there.

Which is why I wait until night. For then, sitting at one of the tables at the restaurant Coconnas, under the quiet arcades of the Pavillon du Roi, one can watch the whole square slip back a few centuries. Everyone comes alive—all the great men and women who walked the same pavement: Marion Delorme, Cardinal de Retz, the Duchesse de Longueville, and especially La Rochefoucauld, who would arrive at the Place des Vosges in the evening, his gouty body trundling ever so cautiously under the arcades as he headed toward no. 5 to visit Madame de Sablé. No doubt, his gaze wandered to no. 18, where more than a decade earlier his former mistress, the Duchesse de Longueville, had watched from her window as Coligny had championed her cause and then died for it. He and the Cardinal de Retz and the Duchesse had joined the Fronde in their younger days, only to end up writing lacerating character assassinations of one another. Now the most defeated and disenchanted man in the world—putting up a front, calling his mask a mask, which is how he hid his sorrows in love, in politics, and in everything else—La Rochefoucauld would arrive here to try to put a less sinister spin on his tragic view of life by chiseling maxim after maxim in the company of friends. "True love is like ghosts, which everybody talks about and few have seen." "If we judge love by the majority of its consequences, it is more like hatred than like friendship." "No disguise can forever hide love when it exists, or simulate it when it doesn't."

I think I hear the clatter of horses' hooves bringing salon guests in their carriage, the brawling and catcalling of hooligans wandering into the square, the yelp of stray dogs, the squeak of doors opened halfway and then just as swiftly shut. I can see lights behind the French windows. Then I must imagine these lights going out, one by one, followed by the sound of doors and of footsteps and carriage wheels on the cobblestones again, not everyone eager to run into anyone else, yet everyone forced to exchange perfunctory pleasantries under the arcades, as some head home two or three doors away or pretend to head home but head elsewhere instead.

An hour later the square is quiet.

On my last evening in Paris, I drop by L'Ambroisie. It's almost closing time. I have come to inquire about the name of the dessert whiskey they had offered us at the end of our previous evening's meal. The waiter does not recall.

He summons the sommelier, who appears, like an actor, from behind a thick curtain. The man seems pleased by the question. The whiskey's name is Poit Dhubh, aged twenty-one years. Before I know it he brings out two bottles, pours a generous amount from one, and then asks me to sample the other. These, it occurs to me, are the best things I've drunk during a week in France. I find it strange, I say, that I should end my visit by discovering something Scottish and not French. One of the waiters standing nearby comes forward and says it is not entirely surprising. "Why so?" I ask. "Had it not been for the Scotsman Montgomery, who by accident killed Henry II during a joust, the Hôtel des Tournelles would never have been leveled and therefore the Place des Vosges would never have been built!"

I leave the restaurant. There are people awaiting taxis outside. Everyone is speaking English. Suddenly, from nowhere, four youths appear on skateboards, speeding along the gallery, yelling at one another amid the deafening rattle of their wheels, mindless of everyone and everything in their path as they course through the arcades. As though on cue, all bend their knees at the same time and, with their palms outstretched like surfers about to take a dangerously high wave, they tip their skateboards, jumping over the curb and onto the street, riding all the way past the cruel Rouillac's house, past the bend around Victor Hugo's, finally disappearing into the night.

Only then can I imagine the sound of another group of young men. They are shouting—some cursing, some urging one another on, still others hastily ganging up for the kill. I can hear the ring of rapiers being drawn, the yells of the frightened, everyone on the Place suddenly alert, peering out their windows, petrified. I look out and try to imagine how the torches of the four swordsmen must have swung in pitch darkness on that cold night in January 1614. How very, very long ago it all seems, and yet—as I look at the lights across the park—it feels like yesterday. And like all visitors to the Place des Vosges, I wonder whether this is an instance of the present intruding on the past or of the past forever repeated in the present. But then, it occurs to me, this is also why one comes to stay here for a week: not to forget the present, or to restore the past, but to forget that they are so profoundly different.

In Tuscany

I count the days. I know that I shouldn't. And I try not to. But I do it all the same, because I'm superstitious and need to dampen the magic each time I'm ready to let go and embrace this dreamy Tuscan landscape whose peculiar spell is to make you think that it's yours forever. That you're here to stay. That time actually stopped the moment you left the highway and drove down a pine-flanked road that steals your breath each time you spot the house whose sole purpose on earth, it seems, is to compress in the space of seven days the miracle of a lifetime. Like a lover who knows he's in way over his head, I niggle and fuss and am all too hasty to find fault with the small things, because the large ones can, with just a few colors and a few tones and the toll of bells all over the valley, easily shame my puny attempts to rehearse the wake-up call that is to take everything away.

So I count the days. Two down, five to go. By this time tomorrow, it'll be three down and four to go. Mustn't forget to plan for the day when I'll have spent more days here than I'll have days left to stay. On that morning, I'll brace myself and remember standing outside this very gatehouse with the gardener while stealing a few seconds from our improvised chat to think of the end. From every hour that goes by, I waste a few seconds to invoke my last day here, the way the ancients tipped their goblets and spilled some of their wine when the harvest was plentiful—to

keep the envious gods quiet. Thus, I shoo the unavoidable by
staring at it all the time. It is also my way of picking up the pieces
I'll be putting together in the weeks ahead. This view of the valley outside Lucca. These candlelit dinners in the garden. And the
litany of names that never seems to end: Monticchiello, Monte-
pulciano, Montalcino, Montefioralle—*Monte*-this and *Monte*-that,
a lifetime of Montes.

It seems ages ago that we sat in our living room one Sunday
evening in New York and leafed through endless catalogs of
farmhouses, which for weeks kept streaming into our mailbox.
Houses with or without swimming pool, with or without cook,
with or without vineyard and/or olive grove, with or without *vista
panoramica*—we wanted *vista panoramica*. And we wanted the
cypresses and the ocher-tiled roofs and the faded brown doors
and rusted hinges, and we wanted a brook—must have a brook—
and all around we wanted *pomodori* (tomatoes) and *girasoli* (sun-
flowers) and fattened *zucche* (squash), the whole thing bathed in
steaming parched fields of rosemary and oregano. We wanted
a swimming pool that looks out straight into infinity. And we
wanted to see the adjoining hills and fields through half-opened
windows whose frames themselves are part of the picture.

The villas came in lavish centerfolds, with informal, whimsical names, each promising bliss by stoking timeless dreamscapes
of an inner Tuscany that all of us, especially those who have read
the Romantics and post-Romantics, secretly cradle in ourselves.
A reader's Tuscany. Eternal.

And then I saw *it*. The house was called Il Leccio. *That* one!
I said. *That* one could—if I let it, if I didn't stand in the way and
if I let my guard down for once—*that* one could change my life,
become my life, turn my life into what I've always, always wanted
and known that life could be, even if for only a week: a life where
everything is life-size, where timeless and time-bound are one
and the same.

A house in Tuscany can help us turn over a new leaf, give us a new life, and stir another us—the us that's crying to step out every morning into a sun-washed, ancient land, an us we always keep on the sidelines, under wraps, forever bottled up like a sluggish genie we don't quite trust or know what to do with or how to please—the basic us that needs basic things but likes them with gusto, the way it likes wines and cheeses, aged and not too pasteurized, but things not too wild either, authentic but refurbished, old but not dated. In Tuscany, the world as we know it turns into a world we all imagine must have been once. *Agriturismo,* this Italian invention that converts farmhouses and barns into expensive rental homes, is the ultimate in fantatourism. It allows us to live as country people—or, more accurately, as rustic, frugal feudal landowners did here in bygone days.

Even our food reflects a country squire's fare. For breakfast we have bread, butter, and peach jam—all of it made no more than a few hundred yards away. At lunch we gorge ourselves on the juiciest tomatoes, seasoned with olive oil, lemon, basil—all from around here. The large, brittle crystals of salt, however, are from Sicily. Very frugal. The wine is of the simplest vintage. Nothing fancy anywhere.

We buy into their world, their customs, their temper, their elaborate kindness, and we want to take intimate, furtive peeks at their history these past eight hundred years. We like to touch the ground and feel how each clod of earth has already been trampled on and held, if not bled on, by other human beings. Here have walked artists, poets, braggarts, and ruthless mercenaries. They drank from the very well our children enjoy throwing pebbles in; they serenaded, brawled, and cursed down the very same alleys where just last night we stood waiting for a table for four.

I am talking to the gardener and getting driving directions. I am headed for Chianti. Someone mentioned Sant'Andrea

in Percussina, near San Casciano, where Niccolò Machiavelli
whiled away his years of exile from his beloved Florence. An unusual place, everyone says, because it personifies unassuming,
ramshackle aristocracy.

As I'm getting directions, I am already earmarking this
morning. The gardener, who probably suspects something like
this is going on in my mind, hands me a sprig of dark sage. "Here,
smell." Tourists have ways of finding mementos in almost anything
a native gives them. He is right. Tuscany is made for these mnemonic earmarks. One comes here to feel that this clear sky, these
small towns and valleys with complicated names, these towers
where Baron So-and-so punished his unfaithful wife or where
Count Such-and-such starved with his children and, as legend
has it, ended up devouring them, this little terra-cotta town that
suddenly rises from nowhere, like a cluttered ziggurat made of
clay, and as suddenly slinks back into a tufted valley mottled by
entire swatches of *girasoli*; that all these are indeed meant to
outlast so many lifetimes that they probably won't change till the
very last minute, when planet Earth runs headlong into the sun.
You want to jot each instant down.

Seven a.m. I like to go out and buy milk and bread. I like the
swish of sandals on wet grass, on the gravel, and on the pebbled
path farther off before I turn and head out on the dirt road. The
shrill cry of birds circling high above the cypress trees. Not a
soul anywhere.

Eight a.m. I'm the first to arrive at the bar. I order an espresso
while the barista gets me a small carton of milk. The next person
to walk in is an American. Has the *Herald Tribune* arrived yet?
Non ancora, signore. The American grumbles as he sits and orders
an espresso as well. Obviously a regular early bird who, unlike
me, is here for an "extended" stay. On my way to get warm bread,
I remember that the baker is always a cuckold in Boccaccio's
tales. Tuscans don't salt their bread. In Dante, eating salted bread
adds bitterness to the wound of exile.

Which reminds me of Machiavelli again. In his famous letter of December 10, 1513, to his friend and benefactor, Francesco Vettori, a disgraced Machiavelli pens an embittered portrait of a squire's life in the countryside. "I am living on a farm," writes the man who can't wait to be recalled to public service in his native city. It is a most anticlimactic portrait of agrotourism by Tuscany's most famous agroexile. He gets up before dawn to snare thrushes with his own hands. Machiavelli, who in the course of his letter drops a hint that he's finished a "little work" on princedoms, goes on to describe how he must first prepare the birdlime he'll need for catching the birds, adding that he knows he must surely look totally ridiculous as he trundles about the country carrying a bundle of birdcages on his back. "I caught at least two thrushes and at most six."

Ten a.m. Must do something useful before the day wears on. Later, there'll be no time or willpower left to do anything. The air is still brisk, and you must hasten the pace before intense sunlight sets in. An entire day's activity squeezed into a few charged, brilliant morning brushstrokes of pure light.

Machiavelli: By this time in the day, he must oversee the tree fellers. He chats awhile with them, taking in his daily dose of their tireless bellyaching, only to turn and bicker with those who purchase firewood but are forever coming up with excuses not to pay. By midday, his monotonous schedule takes him to an inn where he'll chitchat with a few people and then head home for lunch with his family, "eating such food as this poor farm of mine and my tiny property allow."

Eleven a.m. Blinding light suddenly explodes like an overripe, flushed peach that fell on the ground this morning and is succulent to look at and must be eaten on the spot else it spills all over. Light acquires the color of earth and of the buildings around us: the color of clay, eternal ocher.

Noon. The distant peal of bells—reminders of time, of place, of customs that make of this world another world. On the scented, dry earth, how sound carries. Will I be able to stand the peal of a distant church bell elsewhere and not think back on this?

The road to and from the villa has become familiar. I no longer get lost in the house. Part of me likes knowing my way around so soon: it means I've gone native, that I'm settled. But another part of me wishes to remain forever lost, as if I'd just landed here and have days and days to go yet before getting used to anything.

We arrive in the small hamlet of Sant'Andrea, in Percussina, at close to one o'clock. I had expected that it would be as difficult as going back in time, but it was faster to get here than to find a bookshop with an edition of Machiavelli's letters.

One p.m. Two Latin words: *fulgor* (radiance) and *torpor* (lethargy, apathy). At what precise time of the day does *fulgor* finally become *torpor*? Light has already lost its transparency, its whiteness, and slides thickly down the slanted rooftops. People automatically seek out the shade. The sun, as people say here, "gives no truce." A translucent mist rises from the ground and lets everything seen through it sway. The air heaves, but there isn't a draft. How do you describe the intense, overwhelming silence after lunch—if not by invoking the most immaterial of sounds: insects?

Machiavelli: Having had lunch at home, the author of *The Prince* will return to the inn, where he'll seek out the company of the host, a butcher, a miller, and two furnace tenders. But these are no Chaucerian pilgrims. I can just picture these sharp-tongued Tuscans burrowing away from the sun in a dingy inn. "With them," he continues, "I sink into vulgarity for the whole day, playing at *cricca* [a card game] and at backgammon, and then these games bring on a thousand disputes and countless insults with offensive words, and usually we are fighting over a penny and are heard shouting as far as San Casciano." Niccolò Machiavelli couldn't have sunk any lower.

What seems so paradoxical is the degree to which he must have hated everything we have come to love about small, rustic

Tuscan life—from its local color, its people, down to his dingy
home in this dingy hamlet in Chianti. The house is not for sale,
of course, but I can't help myself and am doing something that
comes naturally to every New Yorker. I am secretly prospecting. I
see potential. What if for a price . . . ? I could winterize the place
so that I could come at Christmas, at Easter, during the harvest,
at Thanksgiving—let's face it, year-round. Start a new life. A *vita
nuova*—the title of Dante's earlier collection of poems dedicated
to his beloved Beatrice.

In the mud-ridden, stultifying universe where bad fortune
thrust him, the only solace Machiavelli found was in books. Dante,
Petrarch, Tibullus, Ovid. "When evening comes," he writes, "I
return home and enter my study; on the threshold, I take off my
workday clothes, covered with mud and dirt, and put on gar-
ments that are regal and courtly. Thus fitted out appropriately, I
enter the venerable courts of the ancients, where, graciously welcomed by them, I feed on the food that alone is mine and for which
I was born; where I am not ashamed to speak with them and to
question them about the reasons for their actions, and they, out
of their kindness, answer me. And for four hours at a time, I feel
no boredom, I forget all my troubles, I do not dread poverty, and
I am not terrified by death. I give myself over to them wholly."

And this is what I've always suspected about Tuscany. It is
about many beautiful things—about small towns, magnificent
vistas, and fabulous cuisine, art, culture, history—but it is ultimately about the love of books. It is a reader's paradise. People
come here because of books. Tuscany may well be for people who
love life in the present—simple, elaborate, whimsical, complicated life in the present—but it is also for people who love the
present when it bears the shadow of the past, who love the world
provided it's at a slight angle. Bookish people.

This is how I have come to love Tuscany, the way I love most
things: by drifting ever so slightly from them. I count the days

because I love them too much. I count the days, already knowing that one day I will remember how tactless it was of me to have counted the days when I could so easily have enjoyed them. I count the days to pretend that losing all this doesn't faze me.

But I also know myself and know that I am counting *other* days, days and months when I'll come back and find an old house on a patch of land here and, without too much fussing or too much niggling, I'll begin to make it all my own.

Barcelona

The view from the hotel room on this clear sunny morning belongs to any Impressionist painting. Past the French windows and the fluttering sheers that billow every so often to suggest we'll have yet another temperate late-summer day on the Mediterranean, you step out onto the balcony, lean against the slim banister, and there, right before you, is Barcelona's grand cathedral, La Seu, beaming in the sunlight. It stands at the very heart of the Barri Gòtic, the city's old quarter, the way so many large churches stand in the middle of medieval towns that have lived through too many eras, sprawled too far and seen too much to remember who did what to whom, when, and how. Paris, Milan, London, and Berlin have no longer just grown into imposing centers of culture, tourism, and finance. They are global hypercities. And Barcelona, after nearly four decades under the ruthless dictatorship of Generalissimo Franco, is not just on the rebound. It's on the hypermap and it means to stay there.

From the balcony, where I stand and try to fathom this city that continues to elude my grasp, I can make out the same beggar woman I've been seeing for days now. She is dressed in black and always sits on the steps in front of the cathedral doors, her permanently outstretched, stiffened arm almost grazing the tourists who amble in and out of the narrow entrances. She'll be here, as she probably already has been, for many years, uttering doleful thanks to those who give and to those who don't.

There was a reason for coming to Barcelona, but the reason, as everyone warned me, couldn't have been more far-fetched. I came to look for remnants of my Jewish ancestry in Spain. "Remnant" is the wrong word. I know there are no remnants or even vestiges. But I don't know what else to call what I've come looking for. We go to certain places to find what corresponds to something we half-suspect has long been in us already; the outside helps configure, helps us see the inside better. Without the outside—even an arbitrary outside will sometimes do—some of us may never reach the inside.

According to inherited lore, my ancestors came from various places in Catalonia and Andalusia. I am the first in my family to visit Spain in five hundred years. But, as when I am thinking of billions of dollars, I do not know what five hundred years mean when they're applied to me, to my body, to my living hand, to my mother. Five hundred years is unthinkable.

Here, in Barcelona, in August 1391, the Jewish population was all but wiped out in a brutal pogrom. That was also the year in which huge numbers of Jews around the Iberian Peninsula began, or were forcibly made, to convert to Catholicism. One hundred years later, these new Christian converts—referred to as *conversos* and invariably suspected of being false Christians—were hunted down so systematically by the Spanish Inquisition that, after some two hundred years of dogged persecution, it is fair to say either that more Spaniards today have traces of Jewish blood in them than care to know or that the sweeping eradication of Jewry has nowhere been as thoroughly successful as in Spain.

As for the Jews who refused to convert in 1391, they were expelled from the United Kingdom of Spain by King Ferdinand and Queen Isabella 101 years later, in 1492. Jews who live in Spain today either "returned" centuries after their ancestors' expulsion or are recent arrivals from Eastern Europe, America, and North Africa. But they are grafted Jews, imported Jews. The native Jews disappeared.

Ironically, it is not unusual in Barcelona for people to say they suspect having converso ancestors. There is something bold and somewhat roguish in the admission, as if having Jewish blood were almost a diversion, a fillip in one's ancestral tree. These individuals, to twist Freud's term, are shadow converts, people who extrapolate a Jewish past when perhaps none whatsoever existed. If there is a touch of naughty chic in inventing a Jewish lineage, it's also because the possibility seems either remote or simply irrelevant.

And walking around what used to be the *calle* next to the cathedral, one can easily see why. Except for those Jews who, armed with Michelin guides, desultorily look for a clue they've been warned they'll never find, a Jew wandering in the *calle* is like a species that has been extinct for centuries suddenly turning up in its ancestral plain. Death we can countenance. But extinction is unthinkable. I feel like a time traveler returning to the past to avert the death of his forefathers.

On a "Jewish" tour of Barcelona offered by Urban Cultours, I am shown a path through what was once the *calle mayor*, the larger ghetto, and then to the *calle menor*, the ghetto "annex" nearby. I am shown the place where a Jewish temple may have stood once. Ditto the location of another smaller temple. Then I'm shown the house of a Jewish alchemist. One day a young man knocked at his door asking for a love potion. The alchemist, willing to oblige, brewed the desired philter, not realizing that the young man's beloved, for whom it was destined, was none other than his own daughter. The tale has all the makings of a cross between Boccaccio, Ben Jonson, and *Love in the Afternoon*. The lovers, I am told, lived happily ever after.

Outside the alchemist's house I catch myself looking for what I imagine every Jew secretly hopes to find. I am not a believer, and there is something verging on kitsch in the gesture, but with my hand I feel the right lintel of the door in the hope of touching a telltale indention marking the spot of an absent mezuzah. I know that my guide has seen and understood my gesture, but is tactful enough to say nothing. I-know-she-knows-I-know-she-knows . . . I grew up with such converso antics.

The narrow paths of the Barri Gòtic still promise to lead us somewhere, but as we wander through streets that couldn't be more picturesque, streets that are at once very quiet and, a second later, filled with the sounds of artisans plying and banging away at their manual trades, the "Jewish" tour ends where it began, on the tiny Plaça de Sant Felip Neri. I've come full circle and realize that all I've been shown were might-have-beens. This might have been a temple, this might have been a moneylender's house, this the home of a famed courtesan, this yet another temple. Even the Hebrew inscription along one of the building walls is a reproduction. What is genuine and authentic, however, is the fact that after five hundred years, not a trace of one Jew remains.

To see what Jewish life must have been like in medieval times, I am told to visit the tiny town of Girona, less than an hour's train ride from Barcelona.

But in Girona, the same sights reappear: winding, dark cobbled lanes, a ghetto that has seen its heyday and its hellish days, the dank, cloying smell of clay and cloistered chalk, the sound of a dog barking at noon, the ubiquitous presence of the large cathedral overlooking the old ghetto and the painfully sweet odor of flowers about to go bad. I can smell someone cooking lunch and instantly I know how life could have gone on here. People haven't forgotten about Jews here; they've forgotten that they forgot.

Girona is a gem of a little town: it is a carefully reconstructed, meticulously maintained, thoroughly researched Jewish theme park. Headstones have been brought to the Jewish History Museum from the old Jewish cemetery; inscriptions and dates and a few words in memory of so-and-so and such-and-such happen to bear the exact same names as my great-aunts and -uncles.

But in "re-creating" itself, Girona has broken up alleys, altered its walls, and relandscaped itself, which is more or less what
the inhabitants of Girona had done centuries earlier when they
sought to fend off and pen in their Jews. They tore down walls
and built new ones. Modern planners did not necessarily reverse
the process; they did not restore Girona, but in trying to uncover
a shadow Girona, they've reinvented another. There is as much
historical accuracy as there is naughty chic in this.

Playing fast and loose with memory is not uncommon in Barcelona. By defacing artifacts, we deface memory as well. We do it
every day. Perhaps cities should be held to higher standards, if
only because stones remember for us. We alter stones to alter who
we are.

The cathedral in Barcelona is built on the remains of an old
basilica that was razed in the tenth century, rebuilt in the eleventh,
and rebuilt yet once more on the same site in the thirteenth century. The façade of the cathedral, which is illuminated from the
inside in the evening, is imitation Gothic dating back, not to the
Middle Ages, but to the late-nineteenth century.

There is more. The Plaça Nova, a block or so west of the cathedral, faces the remains of the main entrance to the old Roman
town of Barcino. The walls of that town, like repressed desires,
surface everywhere, above ground, underground, and in a women's
accessories store in the Barri Gòtic. Next to the Plaça Nova is
the Avinguda de la Catedral, a pedestrian esplanade and a totally
modern invention. To create a large public space—beneath which
lies a huge garage—old, presumably tottering buildings built
against the Roman walls were torn down, replaced by a sea of
hardened, dark-gray rectangular flagstone slabs. (These slabs
now pave the entire Barri Gòtic. The original cobblestones and
street gutters have been altogether removed, giving the old city,
including the famed Ramblas, Barcelona's long metropolitan
promenade, a cold, synthetic look. The Ramblas's tiles are slightly

different—but the effect is the same.) In one corner of the Avinguda de la Catedral, a fake Roman arch protrudes from the ancient wall, and a ramp, made to look like a drawbridge that has been let down, leads to a tiny road adjoining the cathedral. The Pont dels Sospirs (Bridge of Sighs) connecting two buildings is also a twentieth-century invention. The whole area begins to loom like one giant bionic space where the old and the new, the genuine and the prosthetic, have been indissolubly fused. The feeling becomes eerie when on some stones of the building that used to house the royal archives of Aragon, abutting the cathedral, one makes out inscriptions written in, of all languages, Hebrew. They are fragments of headstones taken from the Jewish cemetery on the hill of Montjuïc.

This is no mere palimpsest. It is more like a five-part invention by Bach and reminds me of one of a genre of tapas in Barcelona, called *montaditos*, from one of my favorite restaurants, Ciudad Condal. It is made of a slice of baguette rubbed with tomato, on top of which a thin sliver of foie gras has been spread, which is then covered (mounted) by a strip of anchovy, over which is placed a sliced dried date, topped by the tiniest mound of Roquefort cheese. A six-part invention. It's a mess, and you'd never think any of its ingredients would go well together, but it works. And this Barcelona does best. It is reverse archaeology in a city that practices reverse chic in so many ways.

I thought I had discovered an authentic alcove in the small Plaça de Sant Felip Neri. It is a quiet spot, with very few trees, and a tiny fountain whose water spouts ever so placidly. Here, Antonio Gaudí, Barcelona's most touted architect, who died in 1926, used to come to sit and be alone with his thoughts. It is said that he was run over and killed by a trolley on leaving this precise square. And here, I too would return to think of this city that I will never fathom because it plays so many tricks on me. Like an eternal striptease, it takes off with one hand what it puts

back on with another, removing a lie to reveal a far subtler one
and not for a second exposing a swath of truth.

Yet even in this quiet oasis of a square I encountered multi-
layered inventions. The façades of the buildings housing the cop-
persmiths' guild and the shoemakers' guild are not indigenous to
the Plaça itself; about fifty years ago, they were moved from elsewhere in the city and grafted here. As in Girona, the job is seam-
less and well done. Inside one of the façades is a small school
adjoining the Iglesia de Sant Felip Neri. They say a hotel may be
built in this square. Finally, there is the Baroque church itself.
One of its walls still marks the spot where a bomb was dropped
during the civil war. There are those who say that this is where
Franco's henchmen carried out their executions. The wall is riddled with what could only be bullet holes. But you wouldn't know
it. There is no plaque to explain anything. Indeed—and the thought
will never leave me—there seem to be no plaques to speak of in
Barcelona. This is a city that not only toys with its past but also
suffers from willed amnesia. And for good measure, it blankets
itself with hard, gray slabs. Stones do not speak here—or what they
say is altogether garbled, if not silenced.

Barcelonans do not talk about the civil war. They do not remember it, the way they do not really remember their Jews. Yet
these are two of the most harrowing pages in the life of their city.

As with the Ramblas, Avinguda de la Catedral has become
the site of a fringe economy staffed by street performers and an
entire macédoine of freaks and mountebanks. The most popular
are the human statues, part of an international fad. Young men
and women paint their skin silver, white, or copper, put on a costume, and, by freezing their posture for hours, imitate statues,
i.e., imitate the imitation of human beings. Unlike the beggar
lady by the cathedral, they do not thank you when you drop a
coin into their hat; instead, they perform an elaborate, meant-to-
seem-mechanical bow-pirouette that also allows them to stretch

their muscles. The "statue" of Columbus, imitating the imposing statue standing at the foot of the Ramblas, where Columbus looks out to the Mediterranean and over and beyond it toward the New World, will, when you drop a coin, take out his telescope, scan the horizon, then lower his arm, look up again, and resume his timeless posture. Clearly this performance touches a nerve somewhere, for children are always asking their parents to drop more coins into Columbus's bowl. But no one, not the children, not their parents, not the tourists, not the statue of Columbus, much less Columbus himself, could have predicted that the discovery of the New World in 1492 would not only coincide with the departure of all Jews from Spain but would also, by opening new trade routes and new harbors, ultimately spell the ruin of the seaport of Barcelona. That Columbus may have come from converso stock is treated as an apocryphal detail. That the Jewish exodus may have proved disastrous to the Kingdom of Spain, or that Spain, until the death of Franco, had not yet recovered from what could possibly have been its worst blunder in history is something it is probably working on—working through, rather. That Barcelona has finally recovered after five hundred years is, however, the true miracle. That I could live to say it is no minor miracle either, seeing that, but for a fortuitous series of events, my ancestors would most surely have perished in the arms of the Inquisition. I am willing to forgive. And Barcelona is willing to forget.

New York, Luminous

Sometimes I won't go home. I'll leave my office, or an evening party, or a place where I stopped for coffee in the afternoon and, on impulse, find myself taking a long walk. There's nothing I'm really looking to do on these walks, though I could make up errands along the way, and there is no one I'm hoping to meet, though I'd love to run into a friend and be asked to linger over a beer or another coffee. And yet it's really the city I am reaching out for, not people, the city I long to encounter and hold on to for a while before I let go of it, or it tires of me and lets me go my way. The city after a busy day. The city on rainy afternoons. The city when you take a day off, or get up at the wrong hour, or get off at the wrong stop and let yourself wander down unfamiliar streets and suddenly find a movie theater you never thought existed and can't wait to enter. A writer's city; a moviegoer's city; a white-nights city; a sleek, cold, modern metropolis with towering glass buildings that can, within seconds, turn into a diminutive neighborhood with its own invasive, earthy, homespun ethnic foods scenting the cobbled lanes that go back a hundred years and speak of times no one recalls and most invent.

One man understood the secret language of cities and how even sidewalks, like Sirens, can lure us and speak to us: Walter Benjamin, the German Jew who took his own life when escape seemed impossible. He had loved Paris and Berlin, not just for what they were but for the shadows that hovered over them—the shadow of time, the shadow of experience, and of wishdreams, a shadow that touched him like strange intimations from bridges and stonework but that could just as easily have emanated from deep within him and, like a film, left its imprint on the narrow passages and inner courtyards he grew to love so much. Everything he touched and returned to seemed haunted by this inner film, this inner version of a city that seems forever eager to confide in him, to meet him halfway, to love him back, and, in the end, helps him dream up homelands anywhere. Without this illusory film he projected he had no way to connect to, much less touch or love, anything at all.

At dusk, I'll walk up Broadway starting at the imposing Time Warner center overlooking Central Park. Like everyone, I have my choice spots, my private, incandescent nerve centers in the city. I revisit these mini-altars with some apprehension, because if I know that stores and buildings have disturbing ways of vanishing without warning, what I fear more is to watch my old haunts turn from me, or my feelings for them suddenly grow cold.

Today, as I walk past the ghost of so many movie houses that have disappeared on Broadway—the Regency, Cinema Studio, the Embassy, the old Beacon, Loews on Eighty-third Street, the New Yorker, the Symphony, the Thalia, the Riviera, the Riverside, the Midtown, the Olympia—I know I'll earmark a moment to lament their passing. But memory is fickle, and the mind stakes everything on new thrills. Which is what I want on today's walk—new thrills, new vistas, new spots. I want to draw something new from the city, though I don't know what it is yet.

Every walk carves out a new city. And each of these tiny cities has its main square, a downtown area all its own, its own memorial statue, its own landmarks, laundromats, bus terminal—in short, its own focal point (from the Latin word *focus*, meaning fireplace, hearth, foyer, home), warm spot, sweet spot, soft spot, hot spot.

Sometimes, heedless of whatever others on the street will think, I like to stop on one such spot and stand and watch. Watch the prewar buildings with their rows and columns of lighted windows reminding me of a gargantuan periodic table. Watch the crowds hurrying home after work. Watch those who've already been home rush out to the theater wearing their expectant night-life on their faces. Watch the stores that have hours to go before closing. Watch the occasional madman peddle hallelujahs around the American Bible Society building, or bicycling food-delivery boys tear down the sidewalk, or the crowd come out from under-ground, and as ever around Lincoln Square, watch the dazzle of carnival lights in this clamorous, floodlit Milky Way, which, scarcely forty years ago, was a humdrum no-man's-land, thrust like an afterthought between the residential Upper West Side and the Hell's Kitchen of *West Side Story* fame.

The brownstone at number 51 West Sixty-seventh Street no longer stands, but it's the address for *The Apartment*, the film that won an Oscar for best movie of 1960—the old West Side, still mom-and-pop in those days, fringing decency, though barely, a hinter-accent of an English no longer spoken. There C. C. Baxter (Jack Lemmon) rents an affordable apartment from his landlady, Mrs. Lieberman, with old Dr. Dreyfuss next door and his kind, gossiping wife rushing to save Miss Kubelik (Shirley MacLaine) when she swallows too many sleeping pills. "I live in the West Six-ties," says Jack Lemmon, "just half a block from Central Park. My rent is eighty-four dollars a month."

A few blocks north sits Woody Allen–land, where Hannah and her sisters still visit their parents on Thanksgiving each year. Not far away on West End Avenue are Sergei Rachmaninoff's and Edgar Allan Poe's homes. Then, past the Pomander Walk, where Bogie lived, Gershwin's home, and, three block up, Duke Ellington's. Sometimes my hot spots are aligned to the city's own official cen-ters: Columbus Circle, Dante Square, Richard Tucker Square,

Sherman Square, Verdi Square, Straus Park, each dotting the
night, when you happen to fly over New York, like speckled clots
marking the city's mysterious, magnetic erogenous zones.

But New York has its eccentric centers as well—clandestine,
unstable, rival centers—totally my own. Like a midshipman with
a sextant, or a dowser with a rod, or a trained acupuncturist with
his needles, I like to pinpoint the exact coordinates of these
imaginary centers, knowing they are nomadic, whimsical, and as
shifty as an unstable polar star that keeps drifting to confuse the
axis of our planet. And perhaps it's these private, eccentric spots
that I go looking for on my walks. Not faces, not the crowd, not
even the city. This is how our terrifying, spire-studded, Draco-
nian megalopolis called New York City begins secretly to draw
us in; on snowy days, it suddenly shrinks to life-size proportions
to become a Westphalian village; on steamy summer days it acquires a smell, a sallow, flushed Old World face, a human scale, a
fishing hamlet.

In that spellbound moment when we're suddenly willing to
call this the only home we'll ever want on earth, New York lets us
into a bigger secret yet: that it "gets" us, that we needn't worry
about those dark and twisted, spectral thoughts we are far too
reluctant to tell others about—it shares the exact same ones itself,
always has.

And suddenly I realize what this is all about—from Melville,
Whitman, Crane to Lorca, de Chirico, Cummings, Camus—the
miracle of intimacy with a place that may be more in us than it is
ever out there on the pavement, because there may be more of us
projected on every one of its streets than there is of the city itself.

New York may end up being no more than a scrim, a spectral
film that is none other than our craving for romance—romance
with life, with masonry, with memory, sometimes romance with
nothing at all. This longing goes out to the city and from the city
comes back to us. Call it narcissism. Or call it passion. It has its

flare-ups, its cold nights, its sudden lurches, and its embraces. It is our life finally revealed to us in the most lifeless hard objects we'll ever cast eyes on: concrete, steel, stonework. Our need for intimacy and love is so powerful that we'll look for them and find them in asphalt and soot.

It's not steel or concrete we love. Steel and cement are the mordant, the primer over which we apply our wishfilm. Without our wishfilm there is no city. The wishfilm we leave on our walks glistens on the city's hard surfaces like the luminous imprint of fish scales left on a butcher's block hours after the fish was caught, cut, and cooked—outside of time. It still glistens, still pulsates, reaching out to strangers, calling out to them, sometimes long after we're gone. The remanence of our presence, our lingering afterimage on this city—the best in us.

These are my wishfilms:

The wilting city at noon. The city of buses that become beaming *vaporetti* on foggy mornings. The after-hours city at 2:00 a.m. when a cabbie stops and a hasty jitter of underdressed girls pelt the cobbled street with spike heels and are instantly rushed into a club. The city on clammy weekend summer nights when the whir of air conditioners holds vigil on quiet side streets that have all but slipped to the Hamptons. The city on crisp, winter-clear mornings. The old city of splashing fire hydrants—do children still play in the water when time stops and the heat rises and all you long for is a brief rain shower to break the spell? The city holding its breath, gauging the clouds. The city when it finally does rain. The city of long shadows. The city of bridges speckling the night. The noir city of Richard Widmark and Dana Andrews. The city when it hops in NoLIta, TriBeCa, NoHo, NoHar, SoHo, SoHar— the city that has no time for sleep, the city that wouldn't know how to sleep. Fake chill of June nights everyone knows will turn unbearably hot. Fake summer in February when we're all out in T-shirts. Soothing duplicity of Indian summer days—better the illusion of summer than face October this year. Autumn in the city: how quickly we forget our romance with summer. The dreaded winter we all know we love.

Sometimes I go looking for the city as I know it will never be again. Derivative city that fancies itself more in novels and films than on its own sidewalks. My city. The city that reinvents itself by the minute but never knows where it's headed, the city whose enemies love it more than it loves to hate itself. The city that's always compared to Rome—because Rome had to fall one day—but will never be Athens because it's way too young to have a past.

I go looking for this city on my walks. The New York that has no date. Atemporal, unreal, spectral, and luminous.

The city as Walter Benjamin might have seen it had he hurried and crossed the Pyrenees before the Nazis closed in on him. The might-have-been city of Benjamin's might-have-been life. His spirit hovers in its precincts precisely because he never made it. The perduration of ghosts that have never been alive here.

I'll find a bench somewhere, sit down, be with him. Benjamin Square. Benjamin Place. Maybe this is his invisible altar, the ultimate hot spot, the ganglion that always glistens at night before its light fades. From here all things radiate and here they all return. New York's imaginary Place de l'Étoile. Paris's Grand Army Plaza.

At some point I may take the bus. Have I encountered something today? I don't always know. Did I step into an iridescent hot spot where time stopped and I was one with myself and this city? I don't know that either. One never knows. One just stops and stares—this building, that building, this narrow road that makes a strange J-turn and summons up something no flimsier than a fantasy, a would-be shroud behind which lurks the imprint of a life unlived awaiting us. Even the bus could turn out to be a hot spot in disguise. All whisper in this pressing secret language of cities—but I'm not always listening, and I don't always hear, and sometimes I don't understand the words.

I look again but suddenly the narrow road with the fancy J-turn freezes, the buildings are mute, and the bus is just a bus again.

The city is ours to borrow, not to keep, and therefore always on spec; it could any moment give us the slip and disclaim us.

This is my world, this my life. One last glance before I head home. Desperately, I hold out for something, a last try, until something finally trickles to consciousness in the form of a question: *What's in me that keeps wanting something out there?* Which is another way of asking: *What's out there that keeps beckoning something in me?*

I come with this question and I leave with this question. There are no answers. What remains instead is the feeling that the real question is not even a question, but a double-edged plea that says: *Do not take it away. Above all, do not take me away.*

Self-Storage

By the time the Manhattan skyline comes into view toward the end of our summer weekend, the feeling in the car is a cross between cabin fever and combat fatigue, underscored by the dread of being back too soon and the mad, persistent anxiety that the wrong turn might forestall the moment when we trundle into a stuffy, unlighted apartment and unload duffel bags crammed with memories, leftovers, and laundry.

The cranky look on our faces declares the long weekend officially over.

Our home looks exactly as we left it in our last-minute dash to flee the city: unfinished work now glares from my desk, while patched-up arguments, tactfully defused three days ago, are ready to erupt again. Even the food, having come all the way back only to head straight into the garbage, looks tense and baffled. Everyone is tired, sunburned, parched: the least spark, the least harmless quip between one son and another, and the whole family catches fire.

What I want, more than anything now, is a solitary corner to put myself back together again before life picks up where I last left it. But there's never enough time for that, and next weekend and the next after that are already spoken for. I need an extra day; yet the earliest possible one shimmers dimly from faraway October.

I'm sure none of our friends feel this way. Our neighbors at 9A or 9D and the other bright and cheerful families I'll run into will describe their weekends with a spirited *grrr-eat*, which springs at you like an overconfident handshake or a muted growl. And when they'll ask me, I too will try to come up with an exuberant *grrr-eat*, though perhaps a touch less cocksure, if only to suggest I'm merely underplaying the peerless excitement of our weekend. I keep putting the thought away as we look for ticks before washing the children and let them watch their favorite TV show, and as we improvise a makeshift dinner and finally take up the books we'd once started to the sound of a distant foghorn and a crackling fireplace.

But the thought springs back again once I open our door and barefooted take the garbage to the chute at the end of the hallway. Only then does it hit me that this is the first time since Thursday that I've had a moment to myself. Five days, and aside from shaving I haven't even had time to look at my face.

I drag out the walk hoping not to run into any neighbors. I catch myself almost envying the people of 9F and of 9G and their weekends that seem so serene and underwhelmed compared with ours, and how music from 9H and dinners at 9J always sound *grrr-eat-er* than our own. Am I the only person who wishes he could escape his own life for a few hours?

Walking back from the chute, I know I'll stop and wonder about 9I again tonight—9I, an apartment that does not actually exist. Relishing every step of this precious walk, I'll feel as you do in the countryside when a cloud passes in front of the moon and you let every muscle in your body slacken as you beg the clouds to still their course, to hide the moon awhile longer, and in that instant suddenly realize how wonderful it is to be so thoroughly alone.

With imaginary stealth and imaginary keys, I'll enter my imaginary 9I. The place is a mess, of course, because house rules are entirely mine. An old couch has miraculously turned up from my undergraduate days, and next to it are piles of Russian novels

I've been meaning to reread, some of them standing partly opened in upside-down formation like tents bivouacked on a weather-beaten rug, the whole room cluttered with things that don't mind the dust, the mess, or the crackling patter of an old recording of the *Goldberg Variations* on perpetual replay.

This is my universe, no one else's. And in this stupor I'll lift the curtain, look out onto an emptied side street in Manhattan, and, staring blankly at the moon, seek out the one person whose friendship I always neglect and take for granted: me.

With that self I want to spend an entire day each week, an imaginary eighth day that begins when I take out the garbage and ends when I've returned—no one even suspecting that if I look so chipper or am whistling something by Bach or am dying to discuss Russian masters with my wife, it's because, like the moon, I temporarily vanished. I spent a whole day in a sealed, air-conditioned bunker where I've slept late, vegged out, paced about, reread *Oblomov*, brewed coffee, downed all manner of high-cholesterol snacks, thought of no one, missed no one, caught up with the paper, my life, my work, my self, and am now ready to return from an imaginary day off to a world that may never understand that if I end up saying *grrr-eat* to those who'll ask about my weekend, it's because, for a few imagined seconds, and just when I thought Monday was almost upon me, I was finally able to run away from those I couldn't be more grateful to love.

The Buildings Themselves
Have Died

On the Upper West Side, the day couldn't have been brighter, and the view toward Riverside Drive, as I rushed to pick up my twins from school, presaged yet another of those clear, sunlit late-summer mornings unique to Manhattan.

But on Broadway, when we joined the human stream headed uptown, the atmosphere was surreal. An endless procession of people was straggling along the sidewalks, all silent, everyone wearing the purposeful look of zombies who have taken to walking not because it was too beautiful a day to be wasted indoors but because walking is what one does when one is thoroughly numbed. One walks. As I and my children walked.

Holding each boy by his hand, I remembered an identical moment on just such a walk with my mother as we hurried home during a sudden blackout in Egypt in 1956 during the Suez crisis. I wanted to think of how she had handled the moment, wanted to think of the layers of ironies involved now, as I remembered that the same anti-Western and anti-Semitic forces that finally ruined our lives in Egypt would, once again, wearing the vestments of anti-Americanism and anti-Zionism, touch my life.

But I couldn't focus. Other images raced through my mind, images of people being hurled or hurling themselves out of the Twin Towers, while others huddled on windowsills, the whole thing blending with clips of jubilant Palestinians, clapping in celebration.

I held my boys' hands more tightly, for the reason I'd held their hands when we crossed the Brooklyn Bridge once: because it was I who was scared.

From where we stood on Broadway in the West Eighties, there was not a sign, not the slightest trace of what was happening downtown. It would take at least twenty-four hours before the smell of smoldering rubber would finally bring reality home to 110th Street. Meanwhile, disbelief is our way of not seeing more than we are able to take in, our way of inhabiting another world, of allowing versions of a different truth to work their way out of the numberless alternatives fate holds in store for us. Besides, did the word *collapse* really mean *collapse*, or was it just a metaphor, a media buzzword?

As I walk with my children, my mind turns back to another blackout reported, not by the networks, but by Herodotus, when the Athenians emptied their city and massed in all manner of ships and boats, while the Persians who had invaded the abandoned city put the Acropolis to the torch, burning what Athens was most proud of, because in burning it they were torching something in the Athenian soul as well. Those who saw the fire watched in silence and horror, no less helpless than those who watched the repeated images of the airplane boring into the second tower, of the collapsing towers, of the billowing smoke that spelled the end.

And perhaps this is what hurts the most about the fall of the World Trade Center. Not only that so many thousands have died but also that the buildings themselves have died, and that in dying, they have taken away a part of the city, a part of the landscape, and therefore a part of ourselves: that part that looks and gropes around and finds its bearings and knows who it is because of how it carves the earth around it.

I am still thinking of the stunned Athenians the next morning when I take my sons for a bike ride down Riverside Drive. School is closed, and exactly as had happened in my own childhood during the final days of 1956, there is an uncanny air of a miniholiday.

As we ride downstream toward the reconstructed jetty on Sixty-seventh Street, I know what we'll all be looking for. A small crowd has quietly gathered there, everyone straining their eyes toward the island's southern tip.

We are drinking water from our bottles. We still have a long way to go before reaching the reported barricade on Fourteenth Street. A French tourist with his wife and daughter, overhearing me speaking in French to my boys, asks where did the towers stand. Surely he knows, but he asks all the same, the way I am asking myself the same question, just in case we're both wrong and, in our haste to think the worst, had simply overlooked them.

I point to a blotch of white smoke in the distance. "Là-bas."

That's what he feared, he says. Then he confides that they had arrived yesterday. They had planned to take pictures from the observation deck. Now they are taking pictures of a cloud.

And finally I realize why I too am staring at that cloud. I am trying to tell myself that nothing lies behind it, absolutely nothing, but I also know that as soon as this cloud clears up, two large towers will once again stud the southern tip of the island. They're just hidden, the way death hides behind the respirator. We need the illusion of a presence for a while, any presence, even a cloud, before things are taken away from us.

Only then do I begin to suspect what really disturbs me. Our buildings are not even markers for us to know what or where we are. They have something we don't have. They have longevity and timelessness burnished into every steel post. They are built to do one thing: to outlast us, to bear witness, to give us the ultimate illusion that we can parlay our way down generations to come. As a father who lost his son in one of the towers said on television, it's wrong for sons to die before their fathers. It's wrong for our monuments to crumble before their builders.

For an instant, I imagined myself in ancient Greece, asking an Athenian the question the Frenchman had put to me. Where would the temple have stood? Pointing to the Acropolis, the man would have indicated a smoldering mound overlooking his town.

And yet, I find something heartening in this. After the Persian invaders had left Attica, the Athenians rebuilt their temple and made it the marvel that still stands on the Acropolis today. We can and must always rebuild our monuments. As for the barbarians, we know what happened to them.

Empty Rooms

The doors to their bedrooms are always shut, their bathroom always empty. On weekends, when you wake up in the morning, the kitchen is as clean as you left it last night. No one touched anything; no one stumbled in after partying till the wee hours to heat up leftovers, or cook a frozen pizza, or leave a mess on the counter while improvising a sandwich. The boys are away now.

Two decades ago there were two of us in our Upper West Side home. Then we were many. Now, we're back to two again.

I knew it would happen this way. I kept joking about it. Everyone joked. Joking was my way of rehearsing their absence, of immunizing myself like King Mithridates VI, who feared being poisoned and learned to take a tiny dose of poison on the sly each day.

Even in my happiest moments I knew I was rehearsing. Waiting for my eldest son's school bus, standing on the corner of 110th Street and Broadway at 6:20 p.m. while leaning against the same mailbox with a warm cup of coffee each time—all this was rehearsal. Even straining to spot the yellow bus as far up as 116th Street and thinking it was there when in fact I hadn't seen it at all was part of rehearsing. Everything was being logged, nothing forgotten.

When the bus would finally appear, the driver, an impatient Vietnam veteran, would dash down Broadway, either squeaking to a halt if the light was red before 110th or hurtling across to

109th to let some of the students out. The bus, from Horace
Mann, trailed the one from the Riverdale Country School by a
few seconds every evening, with the suggestion that perhaps
something like a reckless race along the Henry Hudson had
taken place between the drivers. I'd remember that, just as I'd
remember the reedy voice of the beggar squatting outside Star-
bucks, or my son's guarded squirm when I'd hug him in view of
the schoolmates who watched from the school bus window.

By late November it was already dark at 6:00 p.m. As always,
coffee, mailbox, traffic. Our ritual never changed, even in the
cold. Together, we'd walk down 110th Street and talk. Sometimes
we needed to buy something along the way, which made our time
together last longer. Sometimes we made up errands to avoid
reaching home too soon, especially after Thanksgiving, when all
three sons and I would walk over to the Canadian Christmas tree
vendors and chat them up about prices. And sometimes I'd tell
my eldest that it helped to talk about the day when we wouldn't
be able to take these walks together. Of course, he'd pooh-pooh
me each time, as I would pooh-pooh his own anxieties about college. He liked rituals. I liked rehearsing. Rituals are when we
wish to repeat what has already happened, rehearsals when we
repeat what we fear might yet occur. Maybe the two are one and
the same, our way to parley and haggle with time.

Sometimes, in late fall, these days, when it's not cold but already dark, and the feel, the lights, and the sound of the city can
so easily remind me of the bus stop at 6:20 p.m., I'll still head out
to 110th Street and stand there awhile and just think, hoping it
might even hurt.

But it never hurts. Partly because I've rehearsed everything
so thoroughly that scarcely an unchecked memory can slip
through or catch me off guard, and partly because I've always
suspected there was more sentiment than feeling in my errands
to 110th Street.

Besides, e-mail and cell phones kept my eldest son, in college, present at all times. And there were his twin brothers, who still lived at home and would continue to do so for two more years, shielding me from his absence. Together the twins and I still walked by the tree vendors on 110th Street and still put off buying anything until it was almost Christmas Eve. Things hardly changed. We removed one leaf from the dining table, my eldest's dirty running shoes disappeared from our hallway, and his bedroom door remained shut, for days sometimes. Life had become quiet. Everyone had space. In the morning, on his way to class in Chicago, he always managed to call. A new ritual had sprung.

Then one day, two years later in September, the twins left as well. Suddenly a half gallon of milk lasts eight days, not just one. We don't buy sausages or peanut butter or stock all manner of cereals that have more sugar than wheat. There is no one to rush home and cook for, or edit college applications for, or worry about when they're not back past 3:00 a.m. No sorting though dirty socks, no mediating the endless bickering about who owns which shirt, no setting my alarm clock to ungodly hours because someone can't hear his alarm clock in the morning, no making sure they have twelve No. 2 pencils, and not just two.

All things slow down to what their pace had been two decades earlier. My wife and I are rediscovering things we didn't even know we missed. We can stay out as long as we wish, go away on weekends, travel abroad, have people over on Sunday night, even go to the movies when we feel like it, and never again worry about doing laundry after midnight because the boys refuse to wear the same jeans two days in a row. The gates are thrown open, the war is over, we're liberated.

Months after they'd left, I finally realized that the one relationship I had neglected for so many years was none other than my relationship with myself. I missed myself. I and me had stopped talking, stopped meeting, lost touch, drifted apart. Now, twenty years later, we were picking up where we'd left off and resumed unfinished conversations. I owned myself.

One evening, while preparing dinner with my wife, I went a step further and realized I had committed the unmentionable: I had stopped thinking of the three persons who are still dearer than life itself. I did not miss them and, stranger yet, hadn't thought of them all day. Is the human heart this callous? Can out of sight, out of mind apply to one's children as well? Really?

I was almost ready to pass the cruelest verdict on myself when I suddenly came across something I could never have foreseen, much less rehearsed. A young couple with twins in a stroller was crossing the street in a rush, precisely where the school bus used to stop after speeding to catch the green light on 110th. As I watched them chat with one of the Canadians at the Christmas tree stall, I suddenly wished I was in the young father's place with my own twins, ten years, five years ago, even last year. We'd buy something warm to drink across the street then rush to say hi to the tree vendors. Now it seemed I'd lost the right to walk up to them.

I envied the couple with the twins. And, as though to prod the knife deeper into the wound, for a moment I allowed myself to think that this is twenty years ago, I've just gotten married, my children are not born yet, and our new, three-bedroom apartment feels far too vacant for just the two of us. I stare at the couple and am thinking ahead for them, or ahead for myself, it's not clear which, picturing the good things that have yet to come, even telling myself that the time for the 6:20 bus lies so very, very far away that it's almost impudent to conjure it up just now.

And then I finally saw things for what they were: the time for rehearsing had already come and gone, just as the boys came and went this Christmas, as the tree vendors will indeed come and go each year—this is how it always is and has been: things come and then they go, and however we bicker with time and put up all manner of bulwarks to stop it from doing the one thing it knows, the best is learning how to give thanks for what we have. And at Christmas I was thankful; their bedroom doors were open again. But I knew, even as I welcomed the flurry of bags and boxes and hugs and yelps, that a small, sly corner of my mind was already dreading and rehearsing that morning in January when they'd all head back to the airport.

Rue Delta

After celebrating what was to be our last Passover seder in Egypt four decades ago, I remember watching all the adults in my family leave the dining table, make their way through a long corridor, and reach the dimly lit family room. There, as happened each year, everyone sat quietly, listened to music, played cards, and invariably put everything aside when it was finally time for the nightly news broadcast on Radio Monte Carlo. I never liked Passover, but this year's, our last in Egypt, was different, so I sat and watched the adults. When it was time for them to converge on the radio, I came up to my parents and told them I wanted to go out for a walk. I knew they were always reluctant to let their fourteen-year-old boy roam the neighborhood streets alone by night, but this was my last time, and the walk was to be, without my knowing it, perhaps, my own version of an aimless, farewell stroll, when you find yourself walking not just to see things for the last time or to take mental snapshots for the benefit of what Wordsworth would have called the "after years," but to get a sense of how something as intimately familiar as rue Delta, with its noises and odors and busy crowds and the sound of surf thudding nearby, could, in less than twenty-four hours, after having watched me grow up, forever cease to exist. It would be like taking a last, hopeless look at someone who is about to die or to become a stranger but whose hand still lingers—warmly—in ours.

We try to imagine how we'll live and who we'll be without them;
we try to foresee the worst; we look around for tiny reminders
whose unsettling reappearance in future years could so easily
jolt us with unexpected longing and sorrow. We learn to nip
memory, like a weed, before it spreads. All along, though, we are
no less puzzled by the loss, which cannot sink in yet, than we'll
be, decades later, when we land on the same street and feel that
coming back doesn't sink in either. No wonder Ulysses was asleep
when the Phaeacians put him down on his native soil. Leaving,
like coming back, is a numbing experience. Memory itself is a
form of numbness; it cheats the senses. You feel neither sorrow
nor joy. You feel that you're feeling nothing.

   After walking out of our building, I automatically headed
toward the coast road, known as the corniche of Alexandria,
which used to be very poorly lit in those years, partly because not
all streetlights worked, but also because President Nasser wished
to foster a wartime atmosphere that kept his countrymen forever
fearful of a sudden Israeli air raid. There was always, during
those evenings in the mid-sixties, a suggestion of an unintended,
bungled blackout, which, far from bolstering morale, simply betrayed Egypt's rapid decline. People always stole streetlamps and
pothole covers; seldom did anyone bother to replace them. The
city simply grew darker and dingier.

   But nighttime in Alexandria, during the month-long feast of
Ramadan, when devout Muslims fast until sundown every day, is
a feast for the senses, and as I walked past the throng and stalls
along the scantly lighted street, I was, as all European-Egyptians
of my generation will always remember, accosted by wonderful
odors of sweetened foods that were not only begging me to grasp
how much I was losing in losing Alexandria, but in their over-
powering, primitive fragrance, also trailed with them a strange
sense of exhilaration born from the presage that, finally, on leaving Egypt, I would never have to smell these earthy smells again,

or be reminded that I had once been stranded in what seemed a blighted backdrop of Europe. I was, as always during those final days of 1965, at once apprehensive, eager, and reluctant to leave; I would much rather have been granted an eternal reprieve— staying indefinitely provided I knew I'd be leaving soon.

This, after all, was precisely how we "lived" in Egypt in those days, not just by anticipating a future in Europe that became ever more desirable the more we postponed it, but also by longing for a European Alexandria that no longer really existed in Egypt and whose passing we were every day desperately eager to avert.

Pascal says somewhere that virtues are sometimes seldom more than a balancing act between two totally opposing vices. Similarly, the present is an arbitrary fulcrum in time, a moment delicately poised between two infinities, where the longing to escape and the longing to return find themselves strangely reversed. What we ultimately remember is not the past but ourselves in the past imagining the future. And, frequently, what we look forward to is not the future but the past restored.

Similarly, it is not the things we long for that we love; it is longing itself—just as it is not *what* we remember but remembrance itself that we love. A good portion of my life at my computer in New York City today is spent dreaming of a life to come. What should my real memories be one day but of my computer screen and its tapestry of dreams? Europeans in Egypt spent so much time thirsting for happiness beyond Egypt that, in retrospect now, some of that longed-for happiness must have rubbed off on Egypt, casting a happy film over days we always knew we'd sooner die than be asked to relive. The Egypt I craved to return to was not the one I knew, or couldn't wait to flee, but the one where I learned to invent being *somewhere else, someone else.*

·

Every reader of my memoir *Out of Egypt* comes face-to-face with a disturbing paradox when I reveal that my Passover night walk comes not in one, but in two versions—and that both, in fact, have been published. In the first version, which appeared in *Commentary* in May 1990, an Arab vendor sells me a falafel sandwich just as I reach the coast road; in the second, published in my memoir in 1995, the vendor hands me a Ramadan pastry and refuses to take any money for it.

In both versions, I stare out at the night sea and nurse the same thoughts vis-à-vis an Alexandria I'm already starting to miss. There is a significant difference, however, between the two versions. In the book, I stand alone. In the magazine, I am walking not by myself but in the company of my brother. Indeed, since I was a rather shy, indecisive boy, it was my younger brother, by far the more daring and enterprising of us two, who was more likely to have come up with the idea of taking such a walk on our last night in Egypt. The notion of eating leavened bread or sweet cakes on the first night of Passover could only have been his, never mine, though I was the atheist, not he.

My brother had a bold, impish side to him. People used to say that he loved things, and that he knew how to go after them. I didn't even know what they meant when they said this. I was never sure I loved anything, much less how to go after it. I envied him.

He liked to get to the beach early enough so as not to miss the sun, the way he liked to eat food while it was still hot. The sun gave me migraines, and as for warm food, I preferred fruit, nuts, and cheeses. I squirreled my food; he delected in it. He liked meats and tangy sauces, dressings, stews, herbs, and spices. I knew of only one spice, oregano, because I would sprinkle it on my steaks to kill the taste of meat.

My brother would kneel before a basil bush and say he liked the smell of basil. I had never smelled basil until he pointed it out to me. Then I learned to like basil, the way I learned to like people only after he had befriended them first, or to mimic them after watching him ape their features, or to second-guess people by watching how he read their minds and said they were liars.

My brother liked to go out; I liked to stay in. On clear summer days, I liked nothing more than to sit on our balcony at the beach house and write or draw in the shade, watching him race along the sun-bleached dunes toward the beaches, never once turning back, going after life, as my father liked to call it.

Years later in New York, when I grew to love the sun, I did so like a tourist, never a native. I never knew whether I loved the sun for its own sake, as he did, or because it reminded me of my summer days in Egypt, where I had always avoided sunlight. I liked the sun from the shade, the way I like people, not by seeking them out, but as though I might any moment lose their friendship and should already learn to live without them. I enter into friendships by scoping out exit doors.

My brother understood people. All I understood were my impressions—which is to say my fictions—of people, as though they and I were alien species, and each had learned to pretend the other was not.

When, after Egypt, we began to take long walks together in Rome, he liked to change our itinerary, roam, get lost, explore; I liked to go on the same walks each time, for they led to any one of three to four English-language bookstores or to places that were already familiar or that had reminded me of something I had read in a book and that invariably harked back, when you searched deep and long enough and made all the appropriate transpositions, to something vaguely Alexandrian—as though, before feeling anything at all, I needed for it to pass through the customhouse not of the senses, but of memory. Walking through Rome without groping for inner signposts or without hoping to create new

"stations" to which I might return at some later date was totally
unthinkable. I wanted my brother to share my joy each time we
repeated a familiar walk or each time it felt as though we were
indeed somewhere more familiar than Rome. Understandably, in
the end, my brother made fun of my nostalgic antics and, having
tired of me, preferred to go out with friends instead.

And yet, though I learned to love my walks without him, I
still owe him so many places I wouldn't have discovered had it
not been for him—just as, when I went back to Egypt in 1995, I
needed to have him present with me all the time, to officiate my
return, else I'd be numb to the experience. Petrarch's walk up
Mount Ventoux would mean nothing unless his brother were
with him part of the way; Freud's visit to the Acropolis would not
cast the dark spell it did without his brother tagging along to remind him of their father; van Gogh's steadfast Theo was always
there to come to his brother's rescue; Wordsworth needed his
sister to accompany him on his return to Tintern Abbey. I needed
my brother the same way.

When I told him in New York one day that I missed our
summerhouse, he reminded me that as a child I was always the
very last to head out to the beach because, as everyone knew, I
used to hate the beach, Mediterranean or otherwise.

It was his sense of irony, especially the one he aimed at me
for hesitating to eat the falafel sandwich on Passover night in the
1990 version of our late-night walk in Alexandria, that I ended
up sacrificing when I decided to kill him off in my memoir in
1995. Of course, he didn't disappear entirely; he came in through
a back door when I found myself borrowing my brother's voice in
the later version, and, with his voice, his love of life and of this
earth and of pastries. Suddenly, I loved the sun though I'd always
shied away from it. Suddenly, I was the one who loved the odor of
stewed meats and the brush of summer heat; I loved people, I
loved laughter, and I loved to lie in the sun and doze off with just

a fisherman's hat thrown over my face, the smell of the beach forever impressed upon my skin, until that smell became my smell as well, the way Alexandria become my own, though I'd never belonged to it, and never wished to. I had stolen his love because I couldn't feel any of my own.

Was I lying then?

A novel, as the history of the genre from Madame de Lafayette through Defoe, Fielding, Dickens, and Dostoyevsky makes abundantly clear, wants to pass for something it is not; it claims to be a history and, as such, narrates events as though they did in fact happen. A memoir, on the other hand, narrates them to read like fiction, which is to say, as though they may never have happened at all. Each borrows the conventions of the other. One tells things as though they were facts, the other as though they were not. A bad memoir may turn out to have a beginning, a middle, and an end. A good novel, like life, sometimes does not.

The distinction between the two is far, far more disquieting than might appear. If writing a memoir is a way of purging the mind of mnemonic deadweight, can lying about these memories or inventing surrogate memories help at all? Does lying actually facilitate such a release, or does it, as should make sense, stand in the way? Or does writing open up a parallel universe into which, one by one, we try to move all our cherished belongings, the way immigrants, having settled in America, invite, one by one, each of their siblings?

Or is lying about one's life precisely what memoirs are all about, a way of giving one's life a shape and a logic, a coherence it wouldn't have except on paper, a way of returning or of rehearsing such a return, the way some of us would like nothing better than to seek out an old flame, provided the reunion remain a fantasy? Is our life incomplete, incoherent, unless it is given an aesthetic finish? Does a literary sensibility foster the very homesickness that a memoir hopes to redeem? Or does being literary entail the possibility of lying, so that once our lies are embedded in the chronicle of our life, there is no way to remove them, the way it is impossible to remove alloy once a coin is minted or chewing gum once you've stepped enough times on it on pavement?

Friends and readers familiar with the 1990 version of our last Seder were stunned to find me taking this farewell night walk by myself in the 1995 version. What had happened to my brother, and why was he not with me on that walk? And, come to think of it, why was he entirely absent from the book? What kind of a memoir was this if you can remove one character, tamper with others, and—who knows—invent many others?

Removing my brother from the evening walk turned out to be embarrassingly easy—almost as though getting rid of him had been a lifelong fantasy. Some last-minute alterations had to be made to accommodate the late-night dialogue with my brother to a silent monologue without him. These changes turned out to be unforeseeably propitious, as happens so frequently when we lose a few pages and are forced to rewrite them from scratch only to find that we've managed to say things we would never have thought of saying, and may have been longing to say but couldn't, precisely because the things we had the good fortune to lose had stood in the way. The long elegiac sentences at the very end of *Out of Egypt*, which reviewers quote, were, in fact, written with one purpose only: to smooth out the ridges left by my brother's disappearance, to elegize him away.

And suddenly I knew, as I touched the damp, grainy surface of the seawall, that I would always remember this night, that in years to come I would remember sitting here, swept with confused longing as I listened to the water lapping the giant boulders beneath the promenade and watched the children head toward the shore in a winding, lambent procession. I wanted to come back to-morrow night, and the night after, and the one after that as well, sensing that what made leaving so fiercely pain-ful was the knowledge that there would never be another night like this, that I would never buy soggy cakes along the coast road in the evening, not this year or any other year, nor feel the baffling, sudden beauty of that moment when, if only for an instant, I had caught myself longing for a city I never knew I loved.

This is not me speaking. It is my brother.

The last sentence, in its original form in *Out of Egypt*, voiced an altogether different sentiment. I had never loved Egypt. Nor had I loved Alexandria, not its odors, not its beaches or its people. In fact, as originally written, this sentence ended with the rather anticlimactic but far more paradoxical words: "I suddenly caught myself longing for a city I never knew I hated." But, by another irony, this statement was not in keeping with the sunny and ebul-lient portrayal of Alexandria I had adopted throughout the book. My brother loved Alexandria; I hated it.

One of my very first readers immediately sensed this disparity between the word *hate* and the city I seemed to love so much, and asked me to . . . reconsider. In light of my affectionate, at times rapturous descriptions of Alexandrian life, wouldn't, perhaps, the word *love* have made more sense?

No one could have been more right. Without a second's doubt, I crossed out the verb "hate" and in its place put down the "love." From hating Alexandria, I now loved it. Easy.

That I was able to settle the matter so blithely, almost by flip-ping a coin, and go from one extreme to the other, means either that I nursed ambivalent feelings for the city or that I could not decide who exactly the speaker was at that very instant: my brother or I. But even if it were my brother's voice speaking through mine, my writing about Alexandria in such fond, sensual precision, and with such a yearning to recapture this or that moment, or to revisit this or that site, may have been an undisclosed desire on my part to be like him, to feel as he did, to stop being the person I was, and, if I could convince others that I had, come to believe it myself.

But there is another confession in store. The night walk on rue Delta on our last night in Egypt, with or without my brother, never did occur. Everyone stayed home that night, morose and worried as ever, saying farewell to the occasional guests who came by and who, despite our repeated pleas, showed up again on the following morning.

My last walk with my brother in Egypt was simply a fiction. As for the moment when, with or without him, I look out to the sea and promise to remember this very evening on its anniversary in the years to come, it too was a fiction. But this fiction grounded me in a way the truth could never have done. This, to use Aristotle's word, is how I *should* have felt had I taken a last, momentous walk that night.

Indeed, one of the very, very first things I did when I returned to Egypt thirty years later was to head out to rue Delta to revisit my grandmother's home. On rue Delta, it kept coming back to me that I hadn't forgotten the slightest thing, which was disappointing but equally comforting. After so many years, I was unable to get lost. I had forgotten nothing. Nothing surprised me. Even the fact that nothing surprised me failed to surprise me. Indeed, I could have stayed home in New York and written about this visit the way I'd written my memoir: at my desk, in front of my computer screen on the Upper West Side. All I kept thinking on returning to Alexandria was: I've read Proust; I've studied, taught, and written about memory, written from memory; I know all the ins and outs of time and of pre-memory, post-memory, para-memory, of place visited, unvisited, revisited; and yet, as I look at these familiar buildings, this street, these people, and realize I am failing to feel anything but numbness, all I can think of is, they're already in my book. Writing about them had made them so familiar, that it was as if I'd never been away. Writing about Alexandria, the "capital of memory," had robbed memory of its luster.

On rue Delta, the way to the sea seemed already paved for me. I began walking down a street that had not changed in thirty years. Even its odors, rising as they once did from street level to my bedroom three flights up, were not strange enough, while the odor of falafel brought to mind a falafel hole-in-the-wall on Broadway and 104th that had frequently made me think of the tiny summertime establishments in Alexandria, whose falafel now, ironically, smelled less authentic in Egypt than the falafel on Broadway.

I had only to look at the way rue Delta led to the shore and I instantly remembered writing the scene about my brother and how he and I had walked there on our last night in Egypt. All I remembered was not what had happened there decades ago, but simply the fiction I'd written. I remembered something I knew was a lie. We had stopped there, purchased something to eat, and then crossed the coast road and heaved ourselves up to sit on that exact same spot on a stone wall along the seafront, watching the Mediterranean by night with its constellation of fishing boats glimmering on the horizon. I could see my brother as he was then and as he is now, gazing at the wild procession of Egyptian chil-dren waving their Ramadan lanterns along the sandbanks, disap-pearing behind a jetty, reappearing farther off along the shore. I tried to remind myself that he was no longer present in the final version of this very scene, that I'd removed him from it and that

I'd sat overlooking the sea by myself. But however I tried to reason with the memory of that first version, he kept popping back on rue Delta, as though his image, like a Freudian screen-memory, or like an afterimage, a shadow memory, no matter how many times I suppressed it, was a truth that was pointless, even dishonest, to dismiss, even though I knew I had never been on that walk with or without him.

Today, when I try to visualize rue Delta by night, the only picture that comes to mind is one with my brother. He is wearing shorts, a sweater slung around his neck, and is headed to the seafront, already savoring the sandwich he is planning to buy at a corner shop called the Falafel Pasha. I have no other memories of rue Delta. Even the memory of my return visit has begun to fade. What I certainly can't remember is the real rue Delta, the rue Delta as I envisioned it before writing *Out of Egypt*. That rue Delta is forever lost.

Afterword

Parallax

I was born in Alexandria, Egypt. But I am not Egyptian. I was
born into a Turkish family but I am not Turkish. I was sent to
British schools in Egypt but I am not British. My family became
Italian citizens and I learned to speak Italian but my mother
tongue is French. For years as a child I was under the misguided
notion that I was a French boy who, like everyone else I knew in
Egypt, would soon be moving back to France. "Back" to France
was already a paradox, since virtually no one in my immediate
family was French or had ever even set foot in France. But
France—and Paris—was my soul home, my imaginary home, and
will remain so all my life, even if, after three days in France, I
cannot wait to get out. Not a single ounce of me is French.

I am African by birth, everyone in my family is from Asia
Minor, and I live in America. And yet, though I lived in Europe
for no more than three years, I consider myself profoundly, ineradicably European—the way I remain profoundly, ineradicably
Jewish, though I have no faith in God, know not one Jewish ritual, and have gone to more churches in a year than I've gone to
synagogues in a decade. Unlike my ancestors the Marranos who
were Jews claiming to be Christians, I enjoy being a Jew among
Christians so long as I can pass for a Christian among Jews.

I am an unreal Jew, the way I am an imaginary European. An
imaginary European many times over.

I spent the first fourteen years of my life in Egypt dreaming and fantasizing about living in Europe. I belonged in Europe; Egypt as far as I was concerned was simply an error that needed to be redressed. I had no love for Egypt and couldn't wait to leave; it had no love for me and did, in the end, ask me to leave. The beauty of Alexandria, of the Mediterranean, of being in a place that history had labored centuries to set in place meant nothing to me. Even the beach couldn't seduce me. If on a November day the totally deserted beaches of Alexandria seemed to belong to me and to no one else on this planet, and if the sea on those magnificently limpid mornings wasn't capable of raising a single ripple, then all I needed to seize the magic of the moment was one illusion: that this beach was not in Egypt but in Europe, and preferably in Greece. Indeed, whenever I saw a beautiful Greek or Roman statue in Egypt, I would automatically think of Greece, not of a Greek statue in Egypt. A Greek statue in Egypt was simply waiting to be taken back to its rightful place in Athens, even if the rightful place for a Hellenistic statue was, in fact, not Athens but Alexandria. A beautiful Mediterranean mansion on the Pacific Ocean is basically asking me to imagine it is—and by extension that I am—in Italy, not in Beverly Hills. If a beach in Egypt reminded me of pictures I had seen of Capri, or if a narrow cobble lane made me think of towns in Provence, the impulse was not to enjoy either spot for what it was—a beautiful place—but as a *simulacrum* desperately yearning to be *repatriated*, i.e., brought back to Europe. This counterfactual circuit, this distortion and dislocation, allowed me to live in Egypt.

When I remember Alexandria it's *not only* Alexandria I remember. When I remember Alexandria, I remember a place from which I liked to imagine being already elsewhere. To remember Alexandria without remembering myself in Alexandria longing for Paris is to remember wrongly.

Being in Egypt was an endless process of pretending I was already out of Egypt.

Not to see this fundamental distortion is to distort memory.

Not to see it as an enduring habit of mind is to forget that I can no longer see anything unless I am able to manufacture or extract similar distortions everywhere. Art is nothing more than an exalted way of stylizing distortions that have become unbearable.

One of my most illuminating and intimate moments in Egypt came with a very old aunt. One evening, as I stepped into her bedroom, I caught her staring at the sea. She didn't turn around but simply made room for me at the window and together we stared at the dark, quiet sea. "This," she said, "reminds me of La Seine."

She told me that she'd once lived very near the Seine. She missed the Seine. She missed Paris. Alexandria had never really been her home. But neither, for that matter, had Paris. Her view of things confirmed my own feelings. Ours was merely the copy of an original that awaited us in Europe. Anything Alexandrian was a simulated version of something authentically European.

By a curious distortion, however, no sooner had I linked our Alexandrian beach with the Seine than I instantly learned to be a bit more forgiving of our beaches in Egypt, and ultimately perhaps to allow myself to nurse some love for Alexandria, because it refracted something irreducibly European. Like my aunt, I needed this detour out to an imaginary Seine and back to a derealized Alexandria to begin to see what stood before my very eyes.

This detour is simply an ancillary version of the distortion I mentioned above. What you see before you summons an imaginary elsewhere. But it is through the conduit of this imaginary elsewhere that you begin to see what's right before you. This kind of detour and distortion simply plays out an inability to connect with the present and consummate experience.

Some of us approach experience, love, life itself, through similar detours. We need to reroute our contempt before realizing that what we have in our hearts is not contempt at all.

Photographers call this *parallax*. Not only are the things before us unstable, but our point of observation is no less unstable.

Because observation itself, like memory, like thinking, like writing, like identity, and ultimately like desire is an unstable gesture, an unstable move. We snap a picture, hoping to gather one picture, when in fact the real picture is an infinite imbrication of unstable images.

Once my family was expelled from Egypt and settled in Europe, we were of course surprised to see that the Europe we mistook for home was no home at all. The alleged repatriation took us to a land that turned out to be more foreign and unfamiliar than what had stood before our very noses for decades in Egypt. Suddenly—and nostalgia is itself a source of many distortions—we became homesick for Alexandria. We grew attached to anything in Europe that reminded us of Alexandria—i.e., we looked for certain spots, for certain moments, inflections of sunlight, vague scents of seawater in Europe that would help evoke our lost Egypt. The detour, so to speak, had come full circle and was about to spiral on to a second remove.

What in Africa had seemed a poor copy of something authentically European became like a sacred original; copies could be found everywhere in Europe, but the original was forever lost. By a curious distortion, going to Capri was not only an attempt to recapture Egypt and, through this detour once again, to grow to accept and, at best, to like what, for better or for worse, was going to be our new home in Italy; it was also an attempt to bring ourselves to cherish the fact that the long-yearned-for repatriation had indeed finally taken place. It was like visiting my aunt's home in Paris and standing at her window and saying to her, "Remember when we stood this way before the sea one evening and dreamed of being in Paris? Well, we're finally in Paris now."

Except that Paris had no value whatsoever unless you invoked—*parallactically*—its shadow partner, Alexandria.

What we missed was not just Egypt. What we missed was dreaming Europe in Egypt—what we missed was the Egypt where we'd dreamed of Europe.

The situation grew infinitely more tangled as soon as I left Europe and moved to America. It's not that Alexandria took a back seat in my mind—it did not; it remained and would always remain, in Lawrence Durrell's words, "the capital of memory." It was just that, as soon as I lost Europe, Europe once again began to exert its pull on my mind, and all the more forcefully now as my *once-imagined Europe* in Egypt doubled into a *now-remembered-Europe* in America. In fact, longing and recollection, yearning and nostalgia, have been confusing their signals so much over the years that I am by now perfectly willing to accept that memory and imagination are twins who live along an artificial border that allows them to lead double lives and smuggle coded messages back and forth.

Parallax is not just a disturbance in vision. It's a derealizing and paralyzing disturbance in the soul—cognitive, metaphysical, intellectual, and ultimately aesthetic. It is not just about displacement, or of feeling adrift *both* in time and space, it is a fundamental misalignment between who we are, might have been, could still be, can't accept we've become, or may never be. You assume you are not quite like others and that to understand others, to be with others, to love others, and to be loved by them, you need to think *other* thoughts than the ones that come naturally. To be with others you must be the opposite of who you are; to read others, you must read the opposite of what you see; to be somewhere, you must suspect you are or could be elsewhere. This is the *irrealis*-mood. You feel, you imagine, you think, and ultimately write counterfactually, because writing speaks this disturbance, investigates it, because writing also perpetuates and consolidates it and hopes to make sense of it by giving it a form.

The German writer W. G. Sebald, who died in 2001, frequently wrote about people whose lives are shattered and who are trapped in a state of numbness, stagnation, and stunned sterility. Given a few displacements, which occurred either by mistake or through some whim of history, they end up living the wrong life. The past interferes and contaminates the present, while the present looks back and distorts the past.

Sebald's characters see displacements everywhere, not just all around them but within themselves as well. Sebald himself cannot think, cannot see, cannot remember, and, I would wager, cannot write without positing displacement as a foundational metaphor.

In order to write you either retrieve displacement or you invent it.

It doesn't matter whether this displacement is recollected or imagined or anticipated. That you can no longer tell the difference may not be just a symptom of the disturbance; it is the cause of it as well. A displaced person is not only in the wrong place, but he also leads or feels he leads the wrong life. This doesn't mean, however, that because he leads the wrong life, or lives in the wrong place, or has acquired a new name, or speaks or writes in a new language, that there is out there a real life or a real home or a true language. Exile disappears the very notion of a home, of a name, of a tongue. The exile no longer knows what he's exiled from.

Let me give a few short parables.

There is a "move" that has become a standing source of humor among my friends. With my friend A, when I go to have dinner at his house on Riverside Drive in Manhattan, it goes something like this. At some point in the evening, as we're watching the sun set and cast the most luminous shades of orange on the clear waters of the Hudson, a lit barge or Circle Line boat will eventually come into view, and A will unavoidably say, to tease me, "Ah, yes, a *bateau mouche*. We must be in Paris."

He's hit home, and I know he knows it, just as he knows I know he knows it. It doesn't matter whether I'm imagining being in Paris or whether I'm remembering Paris—as far as this move is concerned, memory and imagination are interchangeable. You're here, the mind is elsewhere. Or let me put it in somewhat darker terms: *You're not here. But everything else is.*

Or to put it in yet more alarming terms—and this ties directly to a vision of identity that a Holocaust survivor once shared with me—*Part of me*, he said, *never came with me. It never took the ship. It simply got left behind.*

I don't know what this means. But it made an impression on me, and the more I think of it, the more it rings uncannily true: *Part of me didn't come with me. Part of me isn't with me, is never with me.* The French philosopher Merleau-Ponty was fond of evoking the phantom limb syndrome, where amputees feel excruciating pain in a limb that no longer exists on their body. Memory can sometimes bring to the senses things that the senses should realistically no longer be able to feel. But suddenly, because of this mnemonic parallax, of this shadow partner distorting everything, we're reminded of how we are torn in two. Torn from our past, from a home, from ourselves.

This feeling of being cut off from oneself or of being in two places at the same time is as though what was left behind were an amputated limb, something that was cut away from us and was not allowed to travel with us—an arm, a grandparent, a baby brother. Except that the arm did not wither, just as the grandparent or baby brother did not die.

So I am here, across the Atlantic, and this arm is there, beyond Gibraltar. Can I go back and find my arm and put it back where it belongs?

Of course I cannot! But not because the arm wouldn't fit any longer. Or because I've learned to live without it or have acquired a new and even better one, or developed antic ways to work around my missing limb. What is scary is the thought that what I am today may not be a body minus an arm. It may be the other way around. I am just the arm doing the work of the entire body. The body stayed behind. The arm is all that got away. What took the ship was nothing more than an expendable part of me.

I am elsewhere. This is what we mean by the word *alibi*. It means elsewhere. Some people have an identity. I have an alibi, a shadow self.

No wonder I am thinking *bateau mouche* when I am with my friend A. No wonder that dinner at his house feels sometimes provisional and strained, that contact between us is ultimately tangential, unfinished, unfulfilling. Most of me is not even with me now. How can I be with him, in the New World, when I'm not even with myself, when part of me is altogether elsewhere?

With my other friend B, we can give this move an extra twist. As we're walking one Friday evening through a crowded, cobbled main street in Williamsburg, Brooklyn, which, as we instantly both sense, feels so much like a narrow, festive early-summer crowded square in Aix or in Portofino or in San Sebastián, my friend B will look at me and instantly say: "*I know.* For you to appreciate this street *at all*, for you to be on this street you need to think you're over there." He is right. Without this transposition, I cannot experience the present. I need this detour, these twists, these alibis, these counterfactual moves. I need this screen, this scrim, this deception to stand and be in the here-and-now.

With my friend C, add yet a subtler torsion. "For this evening to really reach you, you need to be here thinking you're over there imagining yourself here longing to be over there." Let me explain.

C lives in Paris. A few years ago one September afternoon I felt a terrible longing for Paris—I would have called it homesickness, had Paris really been my home—which, as all my friends know, it's not. I decided to pick up the telephone and call my dear friend C in Paris. After she picked up the receiver, I asked her how was Paris. Her answer did not come as a surprise: "Gray. Paris is always gray these days. It never changes." That of course is exactly how I remember Paris. "And how is New York?" she asked. She missed New York. I missed Paris.

I was not where she was but where she wanted to be; and where I thought I wanted to be was precisely where she was.

When, a few months later, the time came for me to go to Paris, I called her again and said that much as I loved Paris I did not enjoy traveling. Besides, I never found Paris relaxing, I would much rather stay in New York and imagine having wonderful dinners in Paris. "Yes, of course," she agreed, already annoyed. "Since you're going to Paris, you don't want to go to Paris. But if you were staying in New York, you'd want to be in Paris. But since you're not staying, but going, just do me a favor." Exasperation bristled in her voice. "When you're in Paris, think of yourself in New York longing for Paris, and everything will be fine."

With my friend D, add a new torsion. We're sitting on her terrace in Brooklyn having dinner. It's a wonderful dinner—music, food, wine, guests, conversation. As it gets darker, I look over the horizon, and there lies a luminous, magnificent view of the Manhattan skyline just after sunset on a midsummer evening. And it occurs to me that here was something strange indeed, one of the oldest riddles nagging the mind of every New Yorker: Would I rather live in Brooklyn and have the luxury of such a breathtaking view of Manhattan, or would I rather *be* in beckoning, awe-inspiring Manhattan looking over to Brooklyn but never seeing Manhattan?

And then I do what we all do when we're standing in high places. I strain my eyes and ask: Can I see my home from here?

Can I call my old phone number and see who answers? Do I see myself here?

With friend E all this takes a far more complicated turn. E hates nostalgia, he doesn't get it.

You've never loved either Paris or New York or Alexandria.

You love all three.

You hate one because you can't have the other.

You love one but wished you loved the other instead.

You love them all.

You hate them all.

You don't hate, you don't love, you don't even care, because you can't love, can't hate, wished you cared, wished you didn't, don't know, can't tell.

Is there identity in dispersal?

Finally, there is the sixth person in this equation: Me.

In my definition of the move I've been describing, it is not cities that beckon us, nor is it even the time spent in those cities that we long for; rather it is the imagined, unlived life we've projected onto these cities that summons us and exerts its strong pull. The city itself is just a costume, a screen wall, or, as the painter Claude Monet said, an empty envelope. What counts and what never dies is the remembrance of the imagined life we'd once hoped to live.

One more move, call it Me$_1$. When I wanted to buy my eldest son, who is American, his very first history book, I did something that seemed so natural, it almost baffled me: I bought him a book I'd once owned as a child, called *Ma première histoire de France. My First History of France.* When I showed him a richly illustrated scene of the battle of Agincourt, it occurred to me that never once in my life had I decided whose side I was on, the French or the British. On Saint Crispin's day, on whose side was I—a Jew born in Egypt who speaks French, English, and Italian all with the wrong accent?

In fact, I couldn't even decide how to spell the name of the battle: Agincourt with a *g* as the English do, or Azincourt, with a *z* as the French do?

Final, final move. Me₂: I don't even know how to pronounce much less spell my surname: the Turkish way, the Arabic way, the French way, the Italian way, the American way? Come to think of it, even my first name is a problem: Does one call me André the accent on the second syllable, or the American way, with the accent on the first? And how do you pronounce the *r*? Is my name Andrea, Andreas, Andareyah, Andrew, Andy, or is it André as spoken by my father, who named me after a scorned Protestant aunt to spite his family and who spoke my name with a Turco-Italian accent in a family whose mother tongue was neither French nor Italian, not Turkish or Arabic, but Spanish—and even then not really Spanish either, but Ladino?

The fact is, I don't know. I have shadow names, but I don't have a name.

I tried to give an account of all this in *Out of Egypt* when I described my childhood visits to my two grandmothers, both of whom competed for the kind of attention that often passes for love. As was the custom in my preschool years, every day I was taken to one grandmother in the morning and to the other in the afternoon. This was not a difficult thing to do since both grandmothers lived exactly across the street from each other—which is how my parents met. What was a bit more difficult was to visit one grandmother without ever letting the other know that I would later visit, or had just visited, the other. Each was supposed to feel privileged. What thrilled me—correction: what thrilled the adult writer remembering, i.e., imagining, i.e., inventing all this— what thrilled me was the thought that, while visiting the house of one in the morning, I would peek out the window and look at the spot across the street, where I was already anticipating I'd be peeking back later that day. I was in the morning rehearsing what I'd be doing that very afternoon, except that the rehearsal was incomplete unless I could anticipate thinking back on that morning's rehearsal. I was trying to be in both places at one and the same time—like Marcel Proust reading his byline in the newspaper and trying to enjoy both first-person and third-person perspectives. The cunning that had been exercised at first became a precondition for a second form of cunning as well. I was not only disloyal to both grandmothers but I was ultimately shifty with myself as well. And what about the writer who pretends to remember this episode but in reality is making it up, and, by admitting he's invented it, hopes to come clean with this clever loop and access a third-degree alibi?

Perhaps, when I looked out of one grandmother's home in the morning I was trying to second-guess whether I'd be happier across the street later in the afternoon. Or perhaps I was already fearing that I wouldn't be happy there and was thus already sending across the street the comfort I'd need that afternoon. Or perhaps I was afraid that no sooner would I have been taken across than I'd forget the grandmother of the morning, and so I was already sending myself a care package containing the picture of the grandmother I'd left behind that day. Or perhaps it was much simpler: fearing that changing places might change who I was, I was in effect consolidating one identity by grafting it onto the other, except that each was no more stable than the other.

To hark back to Merleau-Ponty's example, I was touching a

leg that within hours would no longer be mine. I was already touching to see what it would feel like to reach for a limb and find nothing.

Caught between remembrance and memory anticipated, the present does not exist. The present does not exist, not because—recall my grandmothers here—the boy in the present already foresees the past before the future has even occurred, or because there are essentially two hypothetical homes, neither of which is the real home, but because the real inhabited space has literally become the street between them, or call it the transit between memory and imagination back to imagination and memory. The loop is the home—the way shame and treachery and the desire to recover from shame and treachery are the primary emotions here, not love. Our intuitions have become counterintuitive, our instincts are thought-tormented, our grasp is counterfactual.

Exile, displacement, and dislocation ultimately induce a corresponding set of intellectual, psychological, and aesthetic displacements and dislocations as well.

Home, if I may invoke the Hebraic tradition, is out-of-home. The word for Hebrew in Hebrew is originally *ibhri*, meaning "he who came from across (the river)." You refer to yourself not as a person from a place, but as a person from a place across from that place. You are—and always are—from somewhere else. You and your alibi are each other's shadow.

This is my home. Unless the counterfactual nerve is stimulated, writing cannot happen. If writing does not force me to displace or reinvent what I believe, what I think, what I like, who I think I am, or where I think I am headed or am writing about—if writing does not unharness me—I cannot write.

There are writers who write by avoiding all fault lines. They sidestep all manner of obstacles, avoid what they do not know, stay away from dark areas, and, wherever possible, end a sentence once they've said all they'd set out to say with it.

Then there are writers who, without meaning to, position themselves right on the fault line. They start out not even knowing what their subject is; they're writing in the dark, yet they keep writing because writing is how they grope, how they light the darkness around them.

For me to write, I need to work my way back out of one home, consider another, and find the no-man's-land in between. I need to go to one André, unwrite that André, choose the other André across the way, only then go looking for the middle André, whose voice will most likely approximate the voice of an André able to camouflage all telltale signs that English is not his mother tongue, but that neither is French, nor Italian, nor Arabic. Writing must almost have to fail—it must almost not succeed. If it goes well from the start, if I am in the groove, if *I come home to writing*, it's not the writing for me. I need to have lost the key and to find no replacement. Writing is not a homecoming. Writing is an alibi. Writing is a perpetual stammer of alibis.

I need to bicker with a language not because language is unsuitable or because I fear I may be unfit for *it*, but because I find myself saying what I think I wanted to say *after*, not before, having said it. Nothing could seem more dislocated. You do not write an outline first and then spill your words on paper; you write because you cannot write an outline. You write the way you do because the other kind of writing is unavailable to you. You write unnaturally not only because you do not have a natural language, but also because writing and thinking have become unnatural acts.

To parody Michelangelo, you do not chip away at marble in order to bring out a hitherto undisclosed statue; testing the marble, hiding its imperfections, covering up mistaken chisel marks *is* the statue.

You write not after you've thought things through; you write to think things through. You chisel in order to imagine what you might have chiseled with better eyes in a better world.

You turn on yourself, and turning gives you the illusion of having a center.

But turning is all there is. Turning is all you have.

Or to put it in different terms: you do not see things; you see double. Better yet: you see that you see double.

You wish to see one thing: instead, you see parallax.

You may want truth; but what you reap is paradox.

I turn on myself not only because I don't know better than to turn on myself; I turn on myself also because it is part of being dislocated and displaced and reversed intellectually and aesthetically to do just that. You don't know whether what you feel is what you feel or what you say you feel, just as you don't know whether saying you feel something is actually a way of saying anything at all about it. You wing it. You hope others believe you. If they believe you, then you might as well copy them and believe the person they believe.

I could sum up exile by saying that I have made writing about exile my home. I could even go on and say that I've built my home not even with words and what they mean but with cadence, just cadence, because cadence is like feeling, and cadence is like breathing, and cadence is heartbeat and desire, and if cadence doesn't reinvent everything we would like our life to have been or to become, then just the act of searching and probing in that particularly cadenced way becomes a way of feeling and of being in the world. Cadenced prose, for all its pyrotechnics, is also a way of hiding that I can't write as plain a thing as an ordinary sentence in English.

But I'm quibbling and these are just words—and saying they

are just words brings me no closer to the sort of truth that so
many of us repair to at the end of the day, because truth, however
unwieldy it is when there's too much of it for anyone to bear or
when there's not enough of it to go around, is still something we
hope goes by the name of home. And that, in exile, is the first
thing you—or they—toss overboard.